When Reality Contradicts Rhetoric

About the authors

Jean-Germain Gros, senior co-author, formerly visiting professor of political science at the University of Ghana, Legon and director of the Missouri-Africa Program, is associate professor of political science and public policy administration and Center for International Studies fellow at the University of Missouri, St. Louis. In addition, Professor Gros is a partner in The Aya Centre, a development consulting organization dedicated to genuine, grassroots, Pan-African development based in Accra, Ghana.

Olga Prokopovych is a law associate at B. C. Toms & Co, Kiev, Ukraine, where she specializes in public and administrative law matters. She earned a masters' degree in public policy administration (MPPA) in May 2003 from the University of Missouri, St. Louis. In Summer 2002, Ms. Prokopovych was an intern at the World Bank.

When Reality Contradicts Rhetoric: World Bank Lending Practices in Developing Countries in Historical, Theoretical and Empirical Perspectives

Jean-Germain Gros
& Olga Prokopovych

Monograph Series

The CODESRIA Monograph Series is published to stimulate debate, comments, and further research on the subjects covered. The Series will serve as a forum for works based on the findings of original research, which however are too long for academic journals but not long enough to be published as books, and which deserve to be accessible to the research community in Africa and elsewhere. Such works may be case studies, theoretical debates or both, but they incorporate significant findings, analyses, and critical evaluations of the current literature on the subjects in question.

Layout by Hadijatou Sy

Printed by Lightning Source

CODESRIA Monograph Series

ISBN 2-86978-159-8 ISBN-13: 978-2-86978-159-7

CODESRIA would like to express its gratitude to African Governments, the Swedish Development Co-operation Agency (SIDA/SAREC), the International Development Research Centre (IDRC), OXFAM GB/I, the Mac Arthur Foundation, the Carnegie Corporation, the Norwegian Ministry of Foreign Affairs, the Danish Agency for International Development (DANIDA), the French Ministry of Cooperation, the Ford Foundation, the United Nations Development Programme (UNDP), the Rockefeller Foundation, the Prince Claus Fund and the Government of Senegal for support of its research, publication and training activities.

Contents

Abstract

This four-part study critically examines World Bank lending policy behaviour in historical, theoretical and empirical perspectives. Its main arguments, each substantiated separately, are three-fold. Firstly, Bank lending policies have been heavily influenced by western development discourses (e.g., modernization theory), which have been mostly neo-liberal but, at times, challenged by counter-worldviews stemming from the harmful impacts of neo-liberalism as policy (e.g., Structural Adjustment Programs) in dependent countries. As a result, although neo-liberalism, is at the core of Bank ideology, it does not always, and single-handedly, determine Bank policy. Where the World Bank is concerned, ideology is expressed in an organizational context and the larger environment of North-South relations, which require the balancing of all three. Thus the study develops a theoretical model of World Bank policy behaviour in Part II based on open systems theory, bureaucratic politics theory (as developed by Allison and Hallerin) and, to a lesser extent, rational choice theory. Much of the gap, between Bank rhetoric and policy reality, is explained theoretically in this section. In Part III the study presents empirical evidence in support of the contention that lending policy continues to follow a familiar pattern, namely, in spite of rhetorical commitment to poverty reduction worldwide, Bank funds do not always go to the world's poorest countries, nor are they used to finance projects that most directly affect the poor in borrowing countries. Finally, in Part IV the study ponders whether the World Bank should be reformed or rethought (i.e., eliminated).

Introduction

Assailed constantly by critics, respected, if not admired, by the western establishment, coveted by mainstream development specialists (especially young economists) eager to make their mark on the world, seen as indispensable by borrowing countries, especially the poorest ones, and imbued with nearly a messianic sense of correctness in purpose, the World Bank is undoubtedly one of the most storied international financial institutions (IFIs) in the world. Like its sister institution (International Monetary Fund), the World Bank leaves no student of the political economy of development indifferent; any conference in which it comes up as a subject is certain to generate very strong feelings—and why not?

The World Bank is the world's largest multilateral development lending institution; its aim, Bank literature claims, is poverty reduction in the Third World.1 Governments look to the World Bank as they grapple with the most basic, yet daunting, challenges of our time: poverty, malnutrition, access to clean water, environmental degradation, infectious disease and ignorance. It is scarcely an exaggeration to assert that whether millions live or die every year hinges on decisions made by the World Bank, among other actors.

Further, a good portion of World Bank funds comes from unsuspecting taxpayers in rich and poor countries alike who do not have a direct say in how unelected, and therefore not popularly accountable, Bank officials dispose of those funds. And, even if they did, they may have neither the time nor the interest nor, frankly, the technical fortitude to investigate how the Bank works. In this environment, it behoves academics and concerned citizens to play a fiduciary role vis-à-vis larger publics. Progressives, in particular, have an important role to play here, inasmuch as Bank lending is not value neutral. For lending, through the conditionalities normally attached thereto, are the means by which the World Bank reorders the economic priorities of borrowing countries, in the process homogenizing the world economy under free-market (or neo-liberal) aegis.

Those who cling, still, to an alternative mode of social organizations (for that's what economies are), and may even hold different philosophical views of what constitute 'development' and 'progress', must challenge neo-liberal hegemony, by bringing evidence to bear on its most pernicious effect: the 'economic horror' it is creating in the Third World.[2] Rather than take the World Bank and other pro-free market international financial institutions at face value, they must question their operating assumptions and subject their data to rigorous analysis. Out of this process of deconstruction, or what sociologists used to call debunking, will hopefully emerge alternative worldviews, which will spur new political struggles, or reinvigorate dormant ones, for greater social justice worldwide. This effort at deconstruction must incorporate three things: history, theory and policy (i.e., empirical) analysis, with the first two providing the framework for understanding the last.

By the same token, critics of the World Bank must avoid caricatures, oversimplifications and polemics. Borrowing governments are not completely at the mercy of the World Bank and do not always do its bidding. Their repertoire of resistance to Bank lending conditionalities may range from outright rejection (e.g., Tanzania under Nyerere in the 1970s) to selective compliance (Russia in the 1990s) to dissimulation and dilatory tactics (much of contemporary Africa). The Bank may be powerful, but its power is neither absolute nor omnipotent. Nor is the World Bank completely oblivious to poverty reduction, improving access to health and education, raising agricultural productivity and the like. As the study will demonstrate, past Bank funding of projects in these areas in the Third World, especially in agriculture, is not trivial. The Bank plays (or can play) a more positive role in the Third World than what might normally be expected, even as it pursues its primary objective of neo-liberal expansion. The challenge is to understand (a) what makes the Bank tilt this way or that (hence the importance of historicizing policy), (b) the limits of Bank actions and (c) variations among borrowing countries in response to Bank policies.

This study is a modest attempt at participating in the endeavour of placing policy in the service of history and theory, so that all three may be better understood. It does so in three ways, each corresponding to the three separate parts making up the study. Firstly, the senior author (who will be referred to, albeit sparsely, in the first personal I) develops in section one an intellectual and policy history of the World Bank from its founding on the ashes of World War II to the present. The main argument, based on the evidence provided by policy history, is that even though the World Bank was committed to free-market ideology (or neo-liberalism) from the beginning, Bank lending policies are not shaped by ideology alone. Secondly, and as a result of the argument in Part I, in Part II I develop a theoretical framework for understanding Bank policy behaviour, including apparent inconsistencies and gaps between rhetoric and reality, that incorporates systems theory, especially, open systems theory, bureaucratic politics and, to a much lesser extent, rational choice theory.

Ideology does not exist in a social vacuum. For an organization like the World Bank, free-market ideology has to compete against the reality of bureaucratic politics and the complexity of the external environment, which is composed in part of sovereign governments whose leaders are in the business, first and foremost, of survival, rather than in the service of the World Bank. Thirdly, Part III, which is a joint effort between the senior author and Ms. Olga Prokopovych, a former research assistant, examines Bank lending in empirical perspective. Much of its novelty lies in the use of Bank, and other establishment organizations, data sets to shed light on this critical question: Does World Bank lending go to the world's poorest countries, and does World Bank lending support projects that, arguably, most directly affect the poor in borrowing countries, namely: health, education, agriculture, water, sanitation and flood protection? We tackled the question because, in its latest (re)imaging the Bank claims to be committed to poverty reduction. We tested this proposition against the evidence of the 1980s, 1990s and from 2000 through 2002, and found that it may well be another instance of *plus ça change, plus c'est la même chose.* Thus the conclusion asks: reforming or rethinking the World Bank?[3]

Introduction

Part I

The World Bank: Institutional Setting, Policy and Intellectual History

The World Bank is actually two organizations: the International Bank for Reconstruction and Development (IBRD), which, was established in the aftermath of World War II to help rebuild war-torn western Europe and Japan, and the International Development Association (IDA), which was established in 1960 to help address what some considered serious flaws with World Bank, then consisting only of IBRD, lending practices.[4] (In this study, I use World Bank, or simply Bank, as a generic term for either IBRD and IDA-related lending activities, unless otherwise indicated.) In addition to the World Bank, there is the World Bank Group. It consists of IBRD and IDA, in other words, the World Bank proper, the International Finance Corporation (IFC), which finances private sector investment, the Multilateral Investment Guarantee Agency (MIGA), which provides insurance against risks, and the International Center for the Settlement of Investment Disputes (ICSID), which helps to settle disputes between foreign investors and host governments. In 2002 the World Bank disbursed 19.6 billion USD for 229 projects in nearly 100 countries, making it the largest multilateral, development lending agency in the world.[5]

The World Bank has two types of lending instruments, one dealing with what Bank documents refer to as investment and the other adjustment. Investment loans finance physical and social development projects, such as roads, ports and water treatment plants, and health care and education, respectively. Investment loans generally have a 5–10-year focus. Adjustment loans, which here include IBRD loans proper and IDA credits, are aimed 'to promote competitive market structures (for example, legal and regulatory reform), correct distortions in incentives regimes [Bankspeak for trade liberalization], establish appropriate monitoring and safeguards [this was one of the lessons of the Asian Financial Crisis of 1998], create an environment conducive to private sector investment... encourage private sector activity...promote good governance (civil service reform), and mitigate short-term adverse effects of adjustment (establishing social protection funds)'.[6]

In other words, adjustment loans support reform regimes aimed at 'correcting macroeconomic distortions', rather than specific projects. Adjustment loans have a one to three-year focus. Since the publication of the Berg Report in 1981, which set the stage for the implementation of Structural Adjustment Programs (SAPs) in many countries, adjustment loans have been

Table 1: World Bank Lending Programs

Conditions	IBRD loans		IDA credits
	FSL*	VSCL**	
Commitment fee	0.85% annually on undisbursed loans for the first four years and 0.75% thereafter	0.75% annually on undisbursed loans	0.0-0.5% on un-disbursed credits (rate set annually)
Front-end fee	1.0 % of loan amount, payable upon loan starting date		None
Lending rate or service charge	Lending rates are product specific and currency specific		0.75%
Maturity	Up to 25 years, including a grace period.		0 years (35 years for countries that receive a blend of IDA credits and IBRD loans), with 10-year grace period

* FSL stands for Fixed-Spread Loans

** VSCL stands for Variable-Rate Single Currency Loan, also known as Variable-Spread Loan (VSL).

Source: IBRD, 'Major Terms and Conditions of IBRD Loans', Washington, D.C., World Bank, February, 2001.

growing in stature, accounting for at least 25 percent of Bank lending. With mounting criticism of the effects of SAPs on the poor, adjustment loans routinely include activities (e.g., health care) that belong to the investment loans category. Table 1 highlights the lending programs administered by IBRD and IDA, including the interest rates charged for, and the duration of, these programs.

The two agencies of the World Bank raise and lend money differently. IBRD raises money on the international financial markets through the issuance of bonds and other transactions; IDA funds come from contributions by individual member states, which, for all intent and purposes, means richer member states. On the lending side, IBRD lends money to support projects while IDA underwrites credits and grants for the same purpose at very low interest rates. Further, IBRD tends to lend money to middle income, resource-rich countries (i.e., those that can pay repay their debt quickly), while IDA focuses on the poorest ones. However, there is more that unites IBRD and IDA than divides them. For example, there is one World Bank president and one board of executive directors, thus making for a unified chain of command.

The governance structure of the World Bank leaves little doubt that it is an instrument of domination by rich countries of poor countries. In theory the World Bank is owned by 184 member countries, in practice a small number of countries exert considerable influence over the Bank. This is because regular operations at the Bank devolve to a 24-member board of executive directors, of whom 5 come from the countries with the largest Bank 'shares' — US, UK, France, Germany and Japan — and represent these countries, even though none has borrowed from the Bank since World War II.[7] Saudi Arabia, China and Russia are also represented by one director each. The remaining 16 members are shared by 176 countries, which necessarily means that they represent groups of countries (formally called constituencies) rather than individual countries. The constituencies represented by these 16 members are not necessarily geographically contiguous, culturally homogeneous, and socio-economically compatible blocs; they are rather arbitrary. Thus, six African countries are represented by Kuwait and Pakistan on the board of executive directors while 44 (African) countries are represented by two people.[8] This raises the question as to how much some of the 16 members of the executive directors board know about the countries they 'represent'. Can they really be effective, given the number of countries for which they are responsible and differences in their socio-economic, political and cultural profiles?

The US is, unquestionably, the most influential member country of the World Bank. By informal agreement, Bank presidents have always been American while managing directors of the International Monetary Fund have always been

European, even though, once again, the World Bank has not lent to the US once. The strength of the US is explained by the fact that each member country of the Bank is allocated 250 'basic votes' (so every country would have a voice) and additional votes based on the size of their economy. Thus, as countries become more prosperous they get (or should get) additional votes. Since the US has by far the largest economy in the world (1/4 of world GDP), it gets more votes than any country. In fact, 'The US is the only country with votes in excess of 15 per cent (of total votes) — the threshold at which any policy or programme can be blocked, making it the only country that has power of veto. The US can, therefore, obstruct any policy it doesn't like.'[9] In other words, the US can prevent any country with which it disagrees (e.g., Iraq under Saddam Hussein after 1990) from borrowing from the Bank; it can also reward countries friendly to Washington with access to Bank lending. The World Bank, in other words, is politicized and is not, therefore, strictly a Bank, as the reader is about to realize.

The history of World Bank lending can be divided into four distinct phases, but no matter the phase, one single ideology has driven Bank policy since its founding: neo-classical, free-market ideology. In the period immediately after World War II (1945-48), phase one, the World Bank was in the reconstruction business in the major combatant countries.[10] The goal then was to help Europe and Japan repair their private capital stock and public infrastructure, and free market means were privileged from the get-go:

> The leaders of the Bank had tremendous faith in private enterprise and private investment as the real engines of growth. Not only did they consider the absorptive capacity of the less developed countries for foreign capital extremely limited, but even the Bank's relatively small contribution to that flow could, in their view, be justified only if borrowing countries followed 'sound' policies. In general, 'sound' policies meant settling outstanding obligations on defaulted pre-World War II bonds, pursuing conservative monetary and fiscal policies, generating sufficient public savings to cover the local currency costs of capital infrastructure projects, and providing a hospitable climate for foreign and domestic private investment. It meant recognizing that oil refineries, steel mills, fertilizer plants, national development banks, and virtually everything but major public utilities ought to be privately owned.[11]

When the Marshall Plan took over the Bank's reconstruction function in 1947, 'development' became its new mantra. However, unlike reconstruction, development was a nebulous, 'slippery' concept; as such, its attainment would be more difficult. In addition, with the focus switched to development, the locus of Bank activities changed. To varying degrees, the western European combatants (and Japan) were geographically compact, industrialized, urbanized, literate, democratic, nascent welfare states, some (e.g., France) with a long tradition of competent public administration. By contrast, the new customers of the Bank, beginning with independent India in 1947, were anything but. In the new environment of industrial development in the Third World, as opposed to reconstruction in parts of the First World, private capital stock, physical infrastructure, political and economic institutions and even human capital had to be built, rather than merely repaired, a challenge made all the more difficult by the legacies bequeathed by colonialism and imperialism, especially in sub-Saharan Africa, namely: artificial states with little anchorage in society, narrow economic bases and the subsequent dependence on one or two cash crops for foreign exchange earnings, authoritarianism, lack of indigenous administrative capacity, etc., all superimposed on the cultural, linguistic, religious and historical differences that may have predated the colonial onslaught. Nevertheless, in the 1950s the World Bank continued to behave as though (re)constructing power plants, steel mills and the like was still its vocation, with due allowance for a change in venue (e.g., from the Rhine to Punjab) and label (from reconstruction to development). So the Bank in the 1950s did not change its taste for gargantuanism and pro-free-market ideology at all, it merely shifted the site for the implementation of its preference.

The practice of lending to big, capital-intensive, industrial projects (what I call here gargantuanism) did not take place in an intellectual vacuum. It coincided with the rise of what would soon become the dominant intellectual thought in the social sciences in the West, especially the United States: modernization theory. According to some of the prominent theorists of that school, the First World had essentially shown the way to the Third World; developing countries were little more than their pre-industrial western counterparts waiting to be propelled toward take off by the engine of technology transfer.[12] In fact, they had certain advantages; their latecomer status allows them to avoid the mistakes of their forebears and adopt, even skip, technologies already developed.[13] Modernization theory generally was, to put it mildly, cool to anything that smacked of tradition, which it saw as inhibiting. The challenge of development was how to overcome the 'obstacles' of tradition and usher in modernity.[14] One of these (i.e., obstacles) was the small, peasant farmer, who was thought to be 'backward' and irrational,[15] in contrast, to the 'progressive' farmer, typically a large landowner and cash crop producer allegedly ready to embrace new technologies.

The extent to which modernization theory (and theorists) influenced World Bank lending practices is beyond dispute. Rita Abrahamsen has argued convincingly that the discourse on development and democracy since World War II, and even before, has been essentially framed by the North and reflects asymmetries in power relations between it and the South.[16] If knowledge is power, as the cliché goes, power is often used to define what is knowledge, and from there it is a short walk to policy 'wisdom'.[17] Too many mainstream American academics moonlighted as consultants to the emerging governments of the Third World, the World Bank and major research organizations (e.g., SSRC), or had their former students reach the highest echelons of state power in their respective countries (e.g., the Berkeley Boys in Indonesia), for the coincidence between modernization theory and Bank policy to have been just that (a coincidence). In any event, there was a confluence of ideas about the meaning and nature of 'development' between the Bank and the intellectual climate of the 1950s and early 1960s, which was reflected in Bank lending. Modernization theory's positive outlook toward the Third World, its equation of development with industrialization, all but provided the theoretical, and yes ideological, backdrop to Bank policy. Modernization theory was in line with neo-classical, free-market ideology, inasmuch as it equated industrialization with 'development' and mainstream modernization theorists (e.g., W.W. Rostow) were unabashedly pro-free-market.[18]

From the mid-1960s through the first half of the 1970s, a shift took place at the Bank, which was certainly not tectonic ideologically speaking, but nonetheless significant in policy terms (ideologies can accommodate challenges without losing their core essence), so much so that it marked the beginning of phase three in Bank lending history, which I shall refrain from labelling just yet. Its most visible manifestation was the creation of International Development Association (or IDA). Whereas in the 1950s Bank funding went to capital intensive and infrastructure, or so-called brick-and-mortar, projects, in the 1960s more attention was paid to 'softer' projects, such as technology transfer in agriculture, public health campaigns, population growth control and mass education. At least two factors accounted for this (apparent) volte face.

More countries joined the United Nations as independent states between 1960 and 1975 than any period of equal length in the 20th century. Many were some of the world's poorest, and the poor inside these countries were illiterate, small, in many cases landless, farmers living in extended families. For this newly discovered group — the majority in many countries — the construction of more power plants would have been, at best, of indirect benefit; in fact, many stood to be harmed, to the extent that electricity generation in those days meant buil-

10

ding dams for hydroelectric power, which flooded valuable farmland. In sub-Saharan Africa, where the World Bank would emerge as the pre-eminent lender, nationalists had sold decolonization to the masses by promising them social services in the new (post-colonial) dispensation.[19] The legitimacy of the post-colonial order came to depend on its ability to deliver education, health services, clean water, rural roads, and the like. Thus, the 'customer' base of the World Bank around 1960 was far different from that of 1945-1948 and even 1955 at the country and sector levels. If it wanted to remain relevant, the World Bank had to at least pretend to be sensitive to the needs of its new clients, and if they wanted to maintain legitimacy, Third Word state elites had to seek funding from the Bank to deliver on their promises, since many lacked the local resources to do so on their own.

The second factor responsible for the shift was the Vietnam War and, more generally, the Cold War. Without falling into the trap of conspiracy theory, it shall be enough to say that many, especially in the United States, thought that the World Bank could do for the Third World what the Marshall Plan had done for western Europe, which was to prevent further gain by the former Soviet Union. As one scholar noted:

> The underlying political rationale behind the bank's poverty focus is the pursuit of political stability through what might be called defensive modernization. This strategy rests on an assumption that reform can forestall or pre-empt the accumulation of social and political pressures if people are given a stake in the system. Reform thus prevents the occurrence of full-fledged revolutions.[20]

'Defensive modernization', to borrow from Ayres, is phase three in the history of Bank lending, and who better to lead the charge than former U.S. Secretary of Defense Robert McNamara, who had by then undergone something of a conversion from Cold War hardliner to practical humanitarian? McNamara may just be the most influential Bank president to date, judging by the resilience of his signature idea—i.e., poverty reduction—which remains the rhetorical stock of the World Bank more than 20 years after McNamara's retirement. McNamara saw poverty in developing countries as a 'blight' and a 'cancer' (interestingly, two of the adjectives American cold warriors often used to describe communism) that posed a threat to 'progressive' governments around the world.[21]

For McNamara also, ever the accountant, poverty could be quantified, in ways all too reminiscent of his tenure at the Pentagon and before that Ford. Thus, the 'absolute poor' were people whose income was 50 USD per annum or below at 1971 prices in the poorest countries, while the 'relative poor' were those with income greater than 50 USD but one-third below the per capita income of the country in which they happened to live. McNamara brought to the Bank like-minded technocrats, mostly development economists (e.g., Hollis Chenery), committed to his vision of poverty reduction.[22] Partly as a result of McNamara's personal commitment, and partly in response to the larger geopolitical factors mentioned earlier, Bank lending to agriculture-related projects, which were also described as poverty-related, increased from 28 to 63 percent, according to one study.[23]

I would be greatly remiss if I did not discuss the shift that took place in the social sciences nearly at the same time as the one that took place at the Bank under McNamara, for, once again, I think the timing of their occurrence to be more than happenstance. Modernization theory was seriously challenged in the 1960s and was nearly run out of the halls of academe by the mid-1970s. Its fall was precipitated, first of all, by the abysmal results of economic development efforts in the Third World. The countries that became independent in the late 1950s did not reach El Dorado a decade or so later, and this includes even those that were rich in natural resources and therefore looked poised for industrial take off following colonial rule. Some descended into anarchy soon after independence (e.g., the former Belgium Congo), while others, perhaps most, experienced some economic growth but with virtually no decline in poverty rates. McNamara's admission could not be more blunt at the board of governors meeting in Nairobi in 1973:

> The basic problem of poverty and growth in the developing world can be stated very simply. The growth is not equitably reaching the poor. The data suggest that the decade of rapid economic growth has been accompanied by greater maldistribution of income in many developing countries, and that the problem is most severe in the countryside.[24]

The root causes of this unwelcome turn of events were the source of much debate between modernization theorists, who tended to attribute Third World rut to endogenous factors, and those who looked outside of this area of the world economy. Modernization theory was on the defensive, for even if one wanted to accept its explanation, it still had to explain its unbounded optimism of only 10 years earlier. The least modernization theorists could say was that they underestimated the resilience of tradition in spite of its lack of rationality, but, for the hordes of idealistic young scholars who went to the Third World to study modernization in action as part of their dissertation requirements, there was more.[25] Tradition did not seem 'irrational' to them at all. On the contrary, the small, peasant farmer, the incarnation of tradition, was a calculating socio-economic agent capable of responding to incentives (or the reverse) and quite knowledgeable of and adaptable to the physical environment,[26] while the 'progressive' farmer, upon whom so much attention and money had been bestowed, turned out to be little more than a rent-seeking interloper, whose interest in farming did not outlive the withdrawal of foreign technology transfer and government and Bank credit.

Having experienced this rude awakening in the course of their field re-search, many returning young scholars, rejected modernization theory, and joined forces with older Left theorists (e.g., Paul Baran, André Gunder Frank, Fernand Braudel, etc.) to create alternative schools, among them dependency theory and world-system theory. Both of these schools rejected the internal dynamic explanation of Third World woes and instead attributed them to the position of poor countries in the international division of labour (i.e., in the periphery instead of at the core).[27] The specialization of poor countries in the periphery in the production of primary commodities, whose prices were generally on the decline, and that of rich countries in the core in the production of finished goods, whose prices were generally on the rise, meant that there was a transfer of wealth from the former to the latter, thanks, once again, to 'unequal exchange'. Third World poverty was the outcome of power relations between core and periphery, which are reproduced in the capitalist world-system. Thus, dependency theory, according to Thandika Mkandawire, 'tended to negate local politics, since the decisive determinant of the policies pursued was the global logic of capitalist expansion, and local politics were an inconsequential sideshow of "petty bourgeois" or "comprador" forces'.[28]

The implication of the dependency school's diagnosis of what was ailing the Third World, or periphery, barely needs spelling out: ending Third World poverty requires countries so classified to break out of the international system. Their continued participation therein could, at best, land them a ticket to dependent development, or intermediary status, not quite among the world's poorest but not quite among the richest either (e.g., Brazil). One of the biggest problems of dependency theory was that the solution proffered 'involved radical "ruptures" which were formulated in such a way as to render them immobilizing by the sheer weight of their implausibility'.[29] In addition, the failure of the Third World to develop was not universal, and development success among the late industrializers (concentrated in Southeast Asia) did not necessarily correlate with size—small countries, like Singapore, were as likely to develop as large ones, e.g., Japan. Finally, there was greater differentiation among countries of the Third World than dependency let on. A theory that captures everything essentially captures nothing. It is a hard to see what Brazil and Gambia have in common other than they are both in the 'Third World', and are therefore structurally 'dependent'.

For the World Bank, the Left successors to modernization theory were completely unsuitable partners. The Left solution precluded even the beginning of a useful dialogue, for its implementation meant the end of the capitalist world-system and the institutions sworn to its upholding (not least the World Bank itself). Nevertheless, the World Bank could not ignore the evidence: the gap between rich and poor countries was increasing virtually worldwide (with the exception of pockets of southeast Asia, and, after 1975, the cash-rich oil states), as was that between rich and poor inside countries. If dependency and world-system theorists did not make the suitable partners that modernization theorists made in the 1950s and early 1960s, they may have had, nevertheless, an impact on Bank behaviour in the 1970s, not because of the acceptability of their remedy but, rather, because of the unassailability of their diagnosis. Furthermore, dependency theorists were not alone in attributing Third World rut to external forces (i.e., core countries and multinational corporations). Other significant voices in the 1970s included the Club of Rome, which raised alarm bells about excessive consumption in the core (or North) and the exhaustibility of Earth's resources, rich but progressive countries sympathetic to the plight of the South (e.g., the Scandinavian countries), environmentalists, the Non-Aligned countries and even some agencies within the UN, all of which were in basic agreement that underdevelopment was not entirely caused by endogenous factors and supported calls for a New International Economic Order (NIEO).

The thrust of NIEO's policy posture was at least three-fold: intensification in the transfer of resources from the North to the South, including technology transfer, so as to level the production and consumption playing field and allow the South to eventually achieve self-reliance, improvement in the terms of trade between North and South and growth with equity, between and within countries. Added to the aforementioned were the conclusion of the Vietnam War, which ended badly for the United States and created the impression that the U.S. was on the decline, and impeachment of American president Richard Nixon. The status quo could not hold, or turn a deaf ear to calls for reform in North-South relations, when East-West relations were thawing. The World Bank would embrace some of the reform proposals but implement them on its own terms, thus undermining more radical policy prescriptions.

In a landmark publication in 1974 edited by one of the economists brought to the Bank by McNamara, the Bank embraced growth with equity as its new mantra, acting, once again, in the larger context of poverty reduction.[30] In its strategic embrace of populism the World Bank was less concerned with the root causes of poverty, least those alleged by Left scholars and activists, than the alleviation of its most visible manifestations. The poor were said to lack 'basic needs', namely, food, shelter, clean water, health care and education;[31] satisfying these needs, therefore, meant reducing poverty. With the help of the Food and Agriculture Organization (FAO), the World Health Organization (WHO) and the International Labor Organization (ILO), various indices of poverty were designed with a view of devising solutions to correct them. For example, nutrition was measured in terms of the calorie intake of individuals. Thus, an adult was said to need so many calories per day in order to be considered properly fed.

Once poverty was quantified, the task then was to turn the abysmal numbers around, thereby reducing poverty itself. Never mind that poverty in any society reflects, first and foremost, asymmetry in the ownership of the means production and lack of popular control over the state, and that what the Bank saw as poverty were rather symptoms thereof. Since poverty is a social condition underpinned by powerlessness at two levels (the economic and political), reducing it requires a fundamental shift in the distribution of productive assets, from haves to have nots, and a redrawing of the boundaries of political power, whereby previously excluded and (or) marginalized groups (e.g., small farmers and women) are given a meaningful, rather than merely symbolic, voice in the affairs of state.

Still, Bank interest in the poor in the 1970s was not all window dressing; the Bank did put significant resources in the rural sector. Through the Rural Integrated Development Project (RIDP), the Bank supported various schemes, often of a multi-sectoral nature. Aid was 'bundled' such that agricultural (seeds and fertilizers), financial (credit to small farmers), infrastructural (feeder roads, abattoirs, water wells) and health (prenatal care, child nutrition, mass vaccination) projects received greater financial support than before. These progressive steps by the Bank must be explained, for they underscore a reality about the institution that critics might be tempted to overlook or dismiss: the World Bank does not always embrace reactionary policies in its relations with Third World countries. Nor are these countries entirely at the mercy of the Bank, as I stated at the outset.

Power is never static in politics, be it domestic or international. At key historical junctures in international relations, power shifts, sometimes in favour of one protagonist sometimes against. Power shifts may sometimes be so subtle as to constitute little more than a window of opportunity for policy change to take place, which then quickly closes until the next swing or cycle. Because the

World Bank has something (money) that its clients need, power may be on its side most of the time, thus the ability of the Bank to negotiate from a position of strength — once again, most of the time As a general proposition, the more desperate the economic situation of a borrowing country, the more vulnerable it is to Bank lending conditionalities (hence the widespread adoption of structural adjustment programs, SAPs, throughout Africa in the 1980s). Conversely, the greater the intensity of external pressure on the Bank, especially if it emanates from core countries, for more borrower-friendly policies, the more accommodating the World Bank will be, at least overtly, to borrower demands (or, perhaps more accurately, pleas).

The early to mid-1970s may have been one of those rare moments when the proverbial stars were in alignment: the World Bank was keen to lend money in support of projects that benefited the poor and Third World countries had gathered enough external support for that to occur. The Keynesian consensus, the ideological underpinning of post-World War II economic reconstruction, which allowed massive public sector participation in the economy to stimulate demand and in the Third World facilitate capital formation, was still holding — albeit barely; developed countries, led by the United States, were still in favour of lending to the Third World, if only to maintain a positive balance of trade by finding new markets for surplus products and prevent debtor countries from going Red;[32] finally, western institutions (banks) were about to become awash in oil money from the oil-producing states, which would render certain countries, hitherto considered poor credit risks, credit-worthy.[33] Finally, commodity prices were generally on the rise between 1970 and 1980; this made Third World commodity producers good credit risks. The 'generosity' on the part of the World Bank and other financial institutions, including commercial banks, would become the bane of the Third World, as they were saddled less than a decade later with crippling debt, the interest payments on which would exert considerable pressure on their foreign exchange earnings and national budgets, thus forcing many to adopt Bank-imposed structural adjustment programs (SAPs).[34] Given the permissive environment for lending in the 1970s by officials from institutions who should have known better, one is almost tempted to conjecture that Third World countries were deliberately lured into borrowing first so their economies could be structurally adjusted later.

In spite of the investment made in poverty reduction, there was a certain banality to Bank lending practices toward this end. In the dispensation of the 1970s the rural poor were no longer 'irrational', but, from the Bank's point of view, continued to be inhibited by 'subsistence' agriculture, low productivity and 'backward' technologies.[35] The rural poor still needed to be 'modernized', but this time around the Bank would bring 'modernization' directly, rather than leave the process to local elites (e.g., 'progressive' farmers), or as a by-product of trickle-down industrialization. Rural development was seen as a matter of raising peasant productivity through better (i.e., 'modern') technologies; rising productivity would, in turn, raise rural income, provided that prices were right. The Bank did not altogether abandon financing big, capital intensive, industrial projects; gargantuanism was evident in Brazil, Turkey, Indonesia and Philippines.

There was absolutely no contradiction between Bank interest in poverty reduction in the 1970s and neo-classical, free-market ideology, for the methods by which the former was to be brought about were supplied by the latter: productivity was the engine of growth, which, in turn, drove development. All three — i.e., productivity, economic growth and development — emanate from changes in relative prices, or market conditions. What had changed, once again, was the locus of Bank lending, from heavy industry to agriculture in some countries and from large, 'progressive' farmers to small, 'subsistence' farmers. In addition, of course, the Bank became a more visible foot soldier in 'defensive modernization', fighting to check the spread of popular and anti-western governments around the world.

There were very few instances in which Bank involvement in the rural sector went to the roots of rural poverty, which in many countries, once again, has to do with the inequitable ownership of land or access thereto, the powerlessness of poor farmers vis-à-vis wealthy local landlords and their lack of voice in the national political process, government corruption by which aid for the poor, such as fertilizers, seeds and credit, is intercepted, customary laws and religious practices that marginalize women as rural producers and protectionist policies in core countries, which limit their markets to commodities from the Third World while at the same time 'dumping' theirs unto the Third World. Since the Bank misconstrued the symptoms of poverty for poverty itself, it ended up trying to deal with the symptoms with no discernible change in the cause. The net result was that rural development projects had very high failure rates, according to the Bank's own admission, and financing of them would virtually disappear from the Bank's ledger from the 1980s onward.

Once again, a policy that emphasized poverty reduction did not necessarily contravene Bank ideology, inasmuch as such a policy relied mainly on market methods and continued to equate economic growth, especially in the agricultural sector, with development. The Bank could claim poverty reduction as its own without abandoning free market ideology; from its point of view, the two were not incompatible. This type of behaviour has been repeated throughout the Bank's history. The World Bank often embraces popular causes, but typically uses (neo-liberal) instruments that undermine their achievement, and eventually abandon these causes altogether once the wind has died down or failure becomes evident. The Bank also has a tendency to be top-heavy (i.e., authoritarian), even in the pursuit of policies that require local participation or democracy, and, worse, even while Bank rhetoric so proffers. Finally, the Bank never takes responsibility for the failure of policies it advocates. Such an outcome is always the fault of governments that did not follow Bank advice to the letter, or the misdeeds of rent-seeking local elites who stood to lose from 'reform'.[36] To the extent that the Bank accepts responsibility for past mistakes, it is always oblique, Nixonesque (as in mistakes were made). In this way, Bank officials escape blame for poorly conceived policies, as do the self-serving (protectionist) actions of countries of the North. Bank interest in the rural poor in the 1970s reflected McNamara's personal interest in limiting the fallout from the Vietnam War and pressure for a New International Economic Order. Improving the lot of the rural poor worldwide, McNamara thought, would decrease their attraction to communism.[37]

The 1970s ended very much as it had begun for most countries: in an atmosphere of economic uncertainty connected in part to the same factor that had shocked the world economy earlier in the decade: oil. The Iranian Revolution of 1979 triggered another round of oil price increases, which aggravated the balance of payment problems of oil importing countries (in other words, most of the Third World). At the same time, the first oil crisis of 1974 had been such a boon to oil producers that it was, almost literally, the lubricant of the world financial system; petro-dollars repatriated from the oil producing countries led commercial banks into a lending binge and since the Bank, as stated earlier, raises money on international financial markets, it too was flushed with money. The deregulation of financial markets from the late 1970s forward also meant that capital could flow in and out of countries with barely a whimper from monetary authorities of ostensibly sovereign governments,[38] a development whose negative repercussions would be felt 20 years later with the Asian financial crisis. The combination of balance of payment deficits, due to deterioration in the terms of trade, the mobility of capital and its concomitant, easy credit, led to a steep rise in borrowing by countries, just at a time when real interest rates on external loans were going up, which further increased the cost of debt servicing. The debt crisis was about to hit oil-importing, Third World countries hard, nay, very hard.

If oil-exporting countries were largely spared the shocks of the 1970s — in some ways they administered them — they were not so fortunate during the recession of the early 1980s. They too suffered as the volume of their (oil) exports fell, due to decreased demand in the core countries, and as the price of oil itself would fall by the middle of the decade, due to excess capacity created in part by the unwillingness of certain OPEC countries to respect production quotas. In Nigeria, for example, oil revenue fell by 80 percent between 1980 and 1985. By the early 1980s all countries in the capitalist world-system — and I mean all — were in varying states of economic difficulties, and so too were the creditors to the most heavily indebted countries. This was especially true of American commercial banks (e.g., Citibank of New York), which had lent huge sums of money to Latin American countries, whose possible default would threaten the financial health of the U.S. banking system at a time when other sectors of the economy (e.g., manufacturing) were meeting stiff competition from abroad, particularly Japan.

Where Africa was concerned, the debt crisis clearly reflected the ills of its economies, hamstrung as they are by overdependence on commodities whose prices are determined outside of the continent, but, as Olukoshi argues, it was also symptomatic of a larger crisis of systemic proportion: that of monopoly capitalism.[39] In particular, and to repeat, the debt crisis was due in part to the lending promiscuity of an earlier era, which was driven by the desire of core capitalist countries, especially the U.S., to maintain positive balances in their trade account. These core countries were exporting their way into prosperity, by encouraging lending to peripheral countries that, in reality, could not afford to borrow and were, in fact, borrowing to import things (e.g., rice in West Africa) deleterious to their own producers. Sooner or later, the chickens (Third World debt) were bound to come home to roost; the problem was, in so doing, they might just destroy the entire barn (finance capital). Once the debt problem surfaced in the Third World, its containment became paramount; it could not be allowed to become contagious.

It was in this context of global recession and anomie that structural adjustment programs (SAPs), which are discussed extensively below, were crafted by the World Bank and IMF. Like modernization theory 30 years earlier, SAPs had their academic inspiration in the West, in particular, the United States. Once again, the work of Rita Abrahamsen is of utility here: the West is the epicentre of the global system and gets to dictate what is development (not to mention democracy) and how to reach it. Karl Marx is also instructive: at any given time the idea of the ruling class is the ruling idea — so it is with countries and geo-economic and cultural blocs. But SAPs were even more dangerous, because, unlike modernization theory, which gained prominence in an era of ideological fermentation and pluralism, SAPs achieved Gramscian hegemony in a world on the verge of unipolarity, ideologically and politically speaking, in which alternatives to market economies would be considered heretic. Dependent countries would have no choice but to agree to SAPs or face collapse, whereas previously they could depend on the former Soviet Union or China.[40]

Like all dominant ideas SAPs had to (re) present reality, for, as Edward Said points out in *Orientalism*, 'there is no such thing as a delivered presence; there is only re-presence, or a representation.'[41] There is no need to mince words here: SAPs recast the economic vicissitudes of the Third World in a way that put the blame squarely on the Third World. The architects of SAPs at the World Bank saw recession and depression in poor countries as prima facie evidence of inherent structural, local pathologies that must be exorcised if sustainable growth is to be experienced. What are these so-called pathologies? In nearly all the cases in which SAPs have been implemented, they are identified as 'profligate' government spending (including on social programs that benefit the poor), 'bloated' bureaucracies, 'distorted' pricing, 'irrational' trade policies, 'overvalued' currencies and 'inefficient' and financially 'burdensome' state-owned enterprises (SOEs) that interfere with normal business activities.[42] (The reader should notice the negative adjectives that pointedly precede each alleged pathology. Curiously, some of these adjectives are often used in reference to the female gender. Thus, neo-liberalism is associated with a more masculine political economy apt at generating growth and 'progress' while the welfare state is given an effeminate spin tending to decline). One must remember, while those who were not yet born should be informed: this was the era of Ronald Reagan, when machismo, honed in in Hollywood movie westerns,[43] held sway in popular culture, diplomacy and economic policy, a posture to which the U.S. may, unfortunately, be returning, but this time with the admixture of religious zeal bordering on crusade in the name of fighting terrorism.

Once the ostensible causes of economic malaise in poor countries are identified, the idea, then, is to help them uproot these causes through a combination of the carrot of financial aid (disbursed in tranches to monitor compliance) and the stick of conditionalities. In Bankspeak, 'Structural adjustment loans (SALs) have generally supported programs designed to increase efficiency economy-wide through changes in pricing and trade policies, in the size and structure of government expenditure and in the extent of the government's controls on productive activities.'[44] In plain language, SAPs involve: reduction in government spending — a non sequitur, since in hard times public sector spending can have stimulating effects on the economy — privatization of state-owned enterprises, deregulation of financial markets, which entails currency devaluation and relaxation of currency controls, liberalization of trade policies, cost recovery of government provided services and overall withdrawal of the state.

All of the aforementioned components of SAPs, directly or indirectly, would have the effect of freeing up resources that so-called structurally adjusted countries could then use to make interest payments on their debt, and, with some luck, draw down principals as well. Meeting their debt obligations would make debtor countries eligible to incur further debt, while insuring hefty transfers of resources (in the form of interest payments) from North to South and profit for the Bank. Eighty-three percent of sub-Saharan Africa's debt is owed to western governments and international financial institutions, such as the World Bank. Between 1982 and 1992, the first decade of SAPs, Africa scraped together 1 billion dollars to service its debt every month — this at a time when drought, famine, civil wars, and the scourge of HIV/AIDS were bearing down on the continent.[45] So who is fleecing Africa?

The 1980s represent phase 4 in the history of Bank lending: whereas in an earlier era Bank funding went to so-called investment, both 'hard' and 'soft', especially 'hard' (i.e., projects), in the 1980s priority was given to adjustment, that is to say, addressing the macroeconomic imbalances ostensibly created by poor government policies, which threatened the success of investment lending.[46] In Bankspeak, 'Structural adjustment loans (SALs) have generally supported programs designed to increase efficiency economy-wide through changes in pricing and trade policies, in the size and structure of government expenditure and in the extent of the government's controls on productive activities.'[47] The World Bank still has investment lending, but 'Both the level and type of the Bank's investment lending may be significantly influenced by the introduction of an adjustment program. The level of investment lending to a country depends, among other things, on the overall policy environment.'[48] In other words, the ability of countries to attract Bank funding for investment, including investment in human development or poverty reduction, depends on their willingness to implement adjustment programs, which in some cases militate against the former. Indeed, structural adjustment programs have been found to exacerbate social inequities, in addition to failing to put countries that have adopted them on the path of sustainable growth.[49]

Gone in SAPs was any demand for a New International Economic Order. This was unnecessary, for the wounds of the Third World were basically self-inflicted; they had nothing to do with quaint issues, such as unequal exchange, worsening terms of trade, exploitation, militarism and imperialism. These were the stuff of politics, and the Bank only dealt in the 'scientific' objectivity of economics. The Bank and its sister institution (IMF) would help borrowing countries achieve the 'discipline' necessary to return to economic rationality. There was almost a religious dimension to SAPs: countries had sinned by pursuing egalitarian and nationalistic policies. Now they were paying for their sins in the forms of staggering debt, recession and even economic collapse. However, all was not lost: they could get back on the road to salvation by adopting SAPs, whose short-term effects might be painful at first but are the necessary price to pay for past indiscretion and future success. SAPs, as Mihevc points out, met every creed of Judeo-Christian theology: sin of excess, propitiatory sacrifice (represented in the bloodletting of SAPs), salvation (return to economic growth). The World Bank was the high priest of this pro-free market, secular theology.

The ubiquity of SAPs at the heart of Bank lending policy in the 1980s is rooted in practical politics on one hand as well as a shift in ideology. Conservative governments swept to power in Great Britain in 1979 and the United States in early 1981. Both Thatcher and Reagan were ideologues, who came to office with a view that 'government was not part of the solution but part of the problem.' For them the welfare state, with its ostensibly cumbersome regulations of business and extensive social benefits, had sapped, respectively, the creativity of entrepreneurs and energy of 'hard working' people, resulting in economic decline on both sides of the Atlantic. What was needed was for government to 'get off the back of the people', and a return to prosperity would be assured. In specific policy terms, this meant business deregulation, cutting taxes and social expenditures, and 'free' trade — in sum, bringing market forces back in.[50] Where Keynesianism, which had hitherto been the consensus on economic policy in the West, saw markets as vulnerable to failures (i.e., recession and depression), and government intervention as necessary to correct these failures, neo-liberalism thought markets to be self-regulating, and government intervention unnecessary, even harmful.

Just as Reagan and his supporters were getting ready to roll back government in the United States, a number of prominent, right-wing magazines (i.e., *Forbes, Fortune, Barrons*) and one think tank (The Heritage Foundation) launched what amounted to full-scale attacks on the World Bank for its pro-'big government' policies in the Third World. Reagan even ordered the U.S. Treasury Department (the American equivalent of a ministry of finance) to investigate the utility of continued U.S. participation in the World Bank. The ensuing review largely vindicated the World Bank, which had in fact always acted to protect US interest; but that the new administration would go to such length to humiliate old friends had to have been unsettling to Bank officials, who were accustomed to thinking that the Bank had bi-partisan support in Washington. U.S. presidents had

22

appointed every Bank president, and the U.S. was (is) the Bank's largest shareholder. As any good Chief Executive Officer (CEO) knows, the unhappiness of the largest shareholder of any company is never to be taken lightly. Reagan and his supporters had put the World Bank on notice. Only a major policy change would silence the critics, who were not in some distant and insignificant Third World capital, but literally within a stone throw of the World Bank.

One must not neglect the importance of ideas to the emergence of SAPs as standard Bank policy. Just as modernization theory and dependency theory were harnessed in the halls of academe first and became the basis (especially modernization theory) for policy later, SAPs had an intellectual history as well; furthermore, SAPs have to be seen as the programmatic arm of a larger ideological shift toward (or more accurately, return to) what would later be called neo-liberalism. The intellectual inspiration to SAPs may be found in the works of conservative economists, such as Milton Friedman, and the school of thought known as monetarism, according to which the money supply is the primary determinant of economic activity.

The thrust of monetarism is adduced in the equation: $MV = PQ$, where M is the money supply and V its velocity. P is the average price level and Q is the quantity of goods and services produced during a given period, say, one year. According to monetarists, as the money supply increases with a constant V, one can expect a corresponding increase in Q, with P remaining constant or going upward only if there is no increase in the quantity of goods and services produced. In other words, a change in the money supply directly affects production, employment and inflation levels. One need not be an economist to uncover the policy implication of monetarism: counter-cyclical fiscal policy, as advocated by Keynesianism, was wrong. The economy could be managed by monetary authorities, i.e., central banks, according to monetary rule, rather than the political instruments of deficits spending in times of contraction to stimulate the economy and fiscal restraints in times of expansion. Besides, argued Friedman in *A Monetary Policy of the United States* by the time fiscal measures are put in place any way, they are usually too late.[51] They had no impact on business cycles.

Monetarism was an important shot across the bow of the post-War (Keynesian) consensus on economic policy, but it was not the only one. In the mid-1970s there developed at the University of Chicago, where Friedman once taught, a strongly pro-free market school in the economics department, some of whose foreign graduates would go on to occupy important positions in their country of origin. Just as Berkeley produced its 'boys' in the 1950s and 1960s,

Chicago did the same in the 1970s, but the latter were of a somewhat different ideological bent than their counterparts on the West coast of the United States. The Chicago Boys were strong advocates of free trade, government deregulation, pro-business and anti-labour. Their political view was more worrisome: they believed in strong, i.e., authoritarian, government that could implement economic reform unpopular with the masses. Chile under military dictator Augusto Pinochet would become the laboratory for the Chicago Boys.

In sum, a number of factors came together in the early 1980s to effect a change in economic development thinking: as stated earlier, the abysmal performance of economies throughout the capitalist world system which called into question the utility of Keynesianism, the rise of monetarism and the Chicago school of free market economics as an alternative paradigm, the election of Ronald Reagan in the United States and Margaret Thatcher in the United Kingdom. In time, neo-liberal ideas would not only gain prominence in the UK and the US, they would spread to such bastions of welfarism as Germany and Sweden, as conservatives ascend to power in these and other countries. Too, pro-free market ideas in core countries would be incorporated in their foreign aid policies, where they had never completely disappeared, thereby allowing for further spread of the gospel.

The World Bank had to respond to the change in political wind if it was to avoid being swept by it. The Bank's ability to do so was probably facilitated by McNamara's decision to step down in 1981 and the choice for his replacement: A.W. Clausen, formerly of Bank of America. I do not want to overestimate the power of Bank presidents, nor, however, do I wish to understate it. (Again, to properly understand the World Bank, it is necessary to synthesize the external environment with the bureaucratic [internal] environment.) The presidency of the World Bank is, undoubtedly, one of the most visible positions in the world. Bank presidents deal with heads of states, key cabinet ministers and politicians, give interviews to journalists all over the world, meet with international bankers and other financiers, and chair the board of executive directors meetings of the World Bank, where policy decisions are made. The ability of any Bank president to handle key constituencies goes a long way toward public perception of the organization, which is important in securing fund. Like him or not, McNamara was a very effective Bank spokesperson. His connection to key lawmakers, especially Democrats, in the United States was solid, even after the imbroglio of Vietnam. By the late 1970s he had generally sold much of the world, and maybe even his colleagues at the Bank, on the idea that the World Bank was in the business of poverty reduction.

Clausen brought to the job a different, and I daresay limited, perspective (he also brought a new corps of neo-liberal, free-trade economists to replace McNamara loyalists, among them Ann Krueger, the original thinker behind the idea of 'rent seeking' behaviour by Third World elites to explain the failure of development, and Deepak Lal, economic advisor to the Research Department of the World Bank and author of the anti-Keynesian *The Poverty of Development Economics)*. Clausen had no direct experience in development,[52] and no demonstrated knowledge of sub-Saharan Africa, where the Bank was the primary creditor to most countries.[53] Clausen's approach to Bank lending was that of a typical banker: In order for the Bank to maintain the confidence of bondholders, projects had to show the promise of solid return on investment, and those that could not (among which were a good many rural projects) would not receive funding.

Rhetorically, Clausen did share McNamara's official commitment to poverty reduction, but 'The key to that poverty reduction lies in raising the productivity of the poor themselves. Welfare programs aimed at the poor without corresponding increases in the productivity of the recipients can only be short-lived and even counterproductive.'[54] In his major addresses as Bank president, Clausen took particular aim at government decisions that, in his view, inhibited growth; presumably, they included the 'welfare programs' (a curious labelling of the development efforts under McNamara) that 'can only be short-lived and counterproductive.' In Clausen's worldview, the key to alleviating poverty was to maintain the flow of international capital to the Third World, reduce barriers to trade and increase industrial productivity (the World Bank had by this time lost interest in rural development). This was nearly a perfect echo of the neo-liberal refrain being heard in parts of the First World.

Under Clausen, the Bank would continue to lend to projects, but more attention would be paid to their return on investment (i.e., profitability) and, just as important, the degree to which they fit the logic of correcting the macroeconomic policies that ostensibly stifled growth and free trade. As the reader will see shortly, these ideas would be incorporated in structural adjustment programs (SAPs). I am not suggesting that, with McNamara at the helm, adjustment lending would not have been embraced by the Bank; on the contrary, I suspect that the pressures in favour of adjustment in the early 1980s were probably too great for anyone to resist. All I am saying is that the passage from McNamara to Clausen facilitated the adoption of SAPs as standard Bank policy and, more generally, it matters who heads the World Bank. McNamara may not have been able to stop the juggernaut of adjustment, but, because of his experience, might have been more in tune to its politics than Clausen was.

Such a sensitivity might have led to the early incorporation into SAPs of 'safety nets' for the poor, which might have avoided the charges levelled at the Bank as the 1980s wore on. Indeed, in sub-Saharan Africa social gains made by the masses in education, health and other areas, as part of the alliance with the African elite against colonialism, were (mis)labelled 'wasteful', and would come in for radical restructuring.

At this point, I should endeavour to bring greater specificity to the analysis by focusing on sub-Saharan Africa, for it was there that SAPs were widely implemented throughout the 1980s and 1990s, and it was there, not surprisingly, that they had their greatest failure. The focus on Africa is important for another reason: even though, by the late 1980, 37 out of 50 countries in sub-Saharan Africa would implement Bank-imposed SAPs—others would implement variants on their own—they were by no means the object of consensus in the region. Development discourse may have been framed and dominated by countries of the North, but dominance does not connote monopoly. Some Africans fought valiantly against SAPs, as they did against other antecedents of domination, such as slavery and colonialism. In particular, African intellectuals and institutions in the 1980s would produce a powerful alternative to SAPs, which would have at least marginal effects on Bank behaviour, if only primarily at the level of rhetoric. Returning to Edward Said, the (re)presentation of reality seldom goes unchallenged. Hegemony produces counter-hegemony, at least temporarily.

SAPs as Alchemy in Africa

In sub-Saharan Africa, the widespread adoption of SAPs in the 1980s as a lending conditionality was intellectually inspired by the publication of *Accelerated Development in Sub-Saharan Africa*, otherwise known as the Berg Report,[55] in 1981. This report was straightforward in the simplicity of its components: it contained a laundry list of what was ailing Africa and proposed remedies. According to the Berg Report, Africa suffered from slow, to negative, growth rates, reduced exports and increased imports. But these problems were not caused by worsening terms of trade, overdependence on a limited range of commodities wrought by colonialism or the policy pursued by developed countries decades earlier that encouraged lending to developing countries by the multilateral institutions and commercial banks; rather, they were caused by overvalued exchange rates maintained by African governments.

One can see from this partial dissecting of the Berg Report, how it 'indigenized' the African development problematic. In addition, argued the report, there was an urban bias in the agricultural policies of African countries, which resulted in low prices to African farmers, especially cash crop producers but also food producers. The prices for food were being kept low, through subsidies and price controls, so urbanites, close as they were to state houses, legislatures, universities and army bases, would have access to cheap staple food and not riot. Peasant farmers, far removed from the centres of power, were less likely to pose an immediate threat to it. On the other hand, low prices to cash crop farmers by government marketing boards were directly responsible for the fall in export revenues. The Berg Report was not entirely original in this diagnosis. Robert Bates had made the same argument at about the same time, as had Michael Lipton in 1977.[56]

The Berg Report also adduced the African crisis to government policy behaviour in the post-colonial era, namely: import-substitution industrialization in which parastatal enterprises loomed 'large', an expansive civil service which also created an expensive public payroll and a 'generous' array of government (what Clausen called welfare) services for which cost recovery was not generally pursued. All of this meant that African governments were living beyond their means. To the extent that the Berg Report made references to the role of external factors in Africa's predicament, it was quickly to reject them in favour of internal ones. The plummeting of commodity prices, high interest rates, protectionism, the decline in the value of the dollar, the unofficial currency of word trade, the burden of debt servicing and the decline, in real terms, of Official Development Assistance (ODA) were peppered over.[57]

The remedies advocated by the Berg Report, which would later be incorporated into SAPs, flowed directly from the diagnosis. Firstly, Berg supported the reinvigoration of the export sector so as to stimulate economic growth and, in the long term, bring about industrialization. The report was clear on this point: 'The agriculture-based and export-oriented development strategy for the development strategy suggested for the 1980s is an essential beginning to a process of long-term transformation, a prelude to industrialization.'58 African cash crop farmers would be given higher prices for their crops, which would give them the incentive to produce more for export. A major plank of the Berg Report was 'Getting Prices Right'. Secondly, to make African goods attractive on the international market, countries should devalue their currency. Also, subsidies should be removed on imported items, which distorted the optimal allocation of resources; restrictions on imports should also be lifted, which would make African producers more competition-conscious and reduce prices for consumers.

The report advocated a wholesale withdrawal of the state from productive activities: state-owned enterprises were to be privatized, and cuts in the size of the civil were be instituted. Users were to be made to pay for government-provided services (cost recovery), such as education and health, and wherever possible private operators were to be encouraged to take over these services. Thus in Cameroon the World Bank would even come to support the privatization of veterinary services; not even animals were to be spared the forces of the market.[59]

There is no doubt that SAPs marked a turning point in Bank history, namely, a return to economic orthodoxy at a time when the capacity of borrowing governments to resist Bank free-market ideology was at low ebb. The forces within the Bank that advocated greater control of Third World economies really won a major battle in the early 1980s, by getting the Bank to move away from funding projects to funding, in reality, policies that the Bank preferred. There was a finality to projects, which limited the Bank's influence in borrowing countries. In concrete terms, once the Bank agreed to finance a hydro-electric dam, a steel mill or an agro-processing plant, it had little say over anything else that borrowers did. But the story was entirely different if Bank funding was made conditional on the implementation of (pro-free market) macro-economic policies. Bank influence, in theory, could increase greatly if lending was tied to policies rather than projects, a fact not lost upon the Berg Report, especially in an era when agreement to Bank-imposed SAPs was being used by other lenders (IMF, London Club, Paris Club, etc.) as a sine qua non for making new loans to, or alleviating the burden imposed by old loans on Third World countries. To be sure, policy-based lending was also risky for the Bank, inasmuch as it gave the Bank paternity over economic reform in countries where such reform was unlikely to bear fruit, But, as always, the Bank had a scapegoat: it could, and did, claim that the failure of SAPs was not due to SAPs themselves but their incomplete implementation by governments that were not committed to reform, or whose officials did not understand rudimentary economics.

The strictures of SAPs were deeply unpopular. They imposed real hardships on Africa's poor, many of whom could not afford the user fees mandated by SAPs on services hitherto provided by the state for 'free'. As a result, consumption dropped, which may have had severe consequences on health, education and the like. In Nigeria, Deji Popoola found that 'ailments that had been declared completely eradicated, such as smallpox and guinea worm in-festation, have reappeared in recent years. Recorded cases of malaria increased from 1.2 million in 1984 to 1.8 million in 1988, and most other notifiable diseases have shown yearly increases as well...'[60] T.O. Fadayomi reported similar findings in education: primary school enrolment stood at 90 percent in Nigeria before SAPs in 1980, by 1987 it had dropped to 64 percent (to be fair, this may have been due not only to the adoption of SAPs but also the drop in the price of oil, which reduced the federal government's revenue).[61] Still in Nigeria, Adebayo Olukoshi wrote that 'During 1980-83, about one million workers were estimated to have been retrenched from the industrial sector.'[62] In Tanzania, according to Haroub Othman and Ernest Maganya: 'the toll on the Tanzanian working people has been clearly evident. Despite slight improvements to the minimum wage, the living conditions of the people have deteriorated even further, and the inflation rate has persisted at its high level.'[63] Zambia abandoned its adjustment program (with the IMF, not the World Bank) in May of 1987 following riots in Lusaka.

The African middle class was not spared. Privatization of state-owned enterprises and cuts in the size of the civil service threw many out of work. For those who were lucky enough to be retained, currency devaluation reduced their real income. In Cameroon civil servants not only experienced this wage cut in disguise, following the devaluation of the Central Africa CFA Franc in January 1994, they also had to agree to nominal cuts in wages, sometimes as much as 40 percent, to reduce government spending as mandated by the World Bank.[64]

To be fair, some aspects of SAPs were positive. The emphasis on increasing producer prices was overdue. African governments (e.g., that of Ghana) had long paid cash crops farmers well below international market prices for their commodities. This would not have been an issue if the gain thus made were ploughed back into agricultural research, infrastructure improvement and replenishment of the price stabilization funds, which state marketing boards were created to manage during the colonial era.[65] But what was taking place in many African countries was the outright appropriation of agricultural surplus value by state officials for occult purposes. The result in countries like Ghana was widespread smuggling (across the border into Côte d'Ivoire) or the exiting of cash crop farming for that of food crops. As a consequence, the Bank rightly concluded, African countries were exporting less and earning less in foreign exchange.

The attempt by SAPs to increase producer prices not only made sense from the standpoint of social justice, it also made economic sense. The problem was, an increase in producer prices, while necessary, was a temporary palliative; it did not, in fact, touch the structure of African economies but, rather, perpetuated their dependence on a handful of commodities for export and foreign exchange earnings. African countries were to export their way out of recession and depression, not by diversifying their production base, but by increasing the volume of the cash crops that had been 'assigned' them by colonialism.

Another problem with SAPs was that by relying almost exclusively on increasing their production of cash crops to earn foreign exchange, African countries risk saturating the world market, thus further depressing the prices of these crops. (Of course, the prices for Africa's exports are decided in London, New York and Chicago, not Cairo, Lagos or Nairobi.) Given that SAPs often required countries to devalue their currency in order to be competitive, one shudders to think at the implication for borrowing countries not only to engage in race to the bottom, in terms of the value of their currency, but also in terms of trying to 'outproduce' one another.

It does not take an economist to figure out that the combination of devalued currencies and commodity saturation is the quintessence of an international buyer's market. Thus, SAPs, even under the best of circumstances, undermined their own success. Besides, devaluation does not only make the goods of the country whose currency has been devalued more attractive on the international market, it also makes import more expensive, therefore, devaluation is often inflationary.66 Africa does not only import luxury cars and other items consumed by urbanites, and true the continent could do without many of these (e.g., second-hand clothes that destroy African textile and garment makers). But it also imports fertilizers, tractors and water pumps, in other words, nearly every input that is needed to increase agricultural output. Currency devaluation is always a mixed blessing and a gamble: whether its effects are beneficial (or harmful) depends on whether the gains from increased sales abroad outweigh the higher prices that must be paid for imported items, assuming that the demand for such items remains constant.

Given the narrowness of Africa's production base, which results in the importation of even the most basic consumer items (flash lights, kerosene lamps, bicycles and even toilet paper), it was more than likely that currency devaluation would negatively affect groups other than the intended target: ostensibly, parasitic middle class and upper class urbanites who lived off the sweat of the African peasantry. Where saturation was concerned, African countries could try to withhold production to bid up prices, but the demand inelasticity of cash crops, unlike that of oil, made the success of that strategy highly implausible, as Félix Houphouët Boigny found out in the case of cocoa in Côte d'Ivoire. In the final analysis, under SAPs African countries would neither be really (re)Structured nor (re)Adjusted; the only letter in the acronym that deserved to be there was the last: countries would be (re) Programmed, lest they would not receive Bank funding, or, for that matter, debt relief from any source. SAPs were the wrong means by which to transform the African crisis into success, hence the analogy to alchemy.

As stated earlier, Africans did not take SAPs lying down. Even the state elites who needed Bank funding (or felt that they did) were sometimes reluctant to be seen as enthusiastic supporters of SAPs. Some sought cover in dissimulation wrapped in pseudo-populism. General Ibrahim Babangida of Nigeria, the sure-footed political Diego Maradona of Africa, called a referendum in 1985 over a proposed IMF loan (the Bank's twin). Nigerians were overwhelmingly against the loan, but the military regime, in an act of apparent self-flagellation, soon implemented, ostensibly on its own, a homegrown SAP. This *pas de deux* would be repeated throughout the 1980s: dependent countries embraced economic orthodoxy one day (to please lenders) and populism the next (to appease their public) as they were hemmed in by opposite forces. There were some genuine dissenters. As seen earlier, Zambia broke with the IMF in 1987. Before that Julius Nyerere, rather than capitulate to Bank and IMF demands, resigned from office, but this only ended one man's illustrious career, not Bank involvement in an African country. Tanzania became a faithful implementer of SAPs under Ali Hassan Mwinyi, and Zambia did return to the IMF/World Bank straightjacket less than one year after freeing itself from it.[67]

In the realm of ideas, the biggest challenge to SAPs was by African intellectuals working through the UN Economic Commission for Africa (ECA) under its director, Adebayo Adedeji. In 1986 the United Nations launched the Program of Action for African Economic Recovery and Development (UNPAAERD). This was a five-year program aimed at putting Africa back on the path of economic recovery, and it was separate from the other programs (including SAPs) being pursued by other multilateral institutions. (For readers who may not know: the World Bank is formally a UN agency but has long achieved de facto independence from the UN. Except for when it thinks association with the UN is likely to be to its benefit, the World Bank almost never mentions its relationship to the UN.) In 1988 the United Nations Development Program (UNDP) and the World Bank issued a joint report meant to coincide with the mid-term report of the UNPAAERD. The UNDP/World Bank report, Africa's Adjustment and Growth in the 1980s, asserted that Africa was on its way to economic recovery, and that countries that had implemented SAPs were growing faster than those that had not. This finding flatly contradicted the mid-term review of the UNPAAERD, as well as the finding of a major study, edited by the ECA director, which 'came to the conclusion that the stabilization and structural adjustment programmes proposed to Africa by IMF and World Bank have had and are likely to continue to have very limited success.'[68]

The ECA became a major rhetorical thorn on the side of the World Bank, especially after it published African Alternative Framework to Structural Adjustment Programmes (AAF-SAP). This study scored a direct hit on SAPs and Bank and UNDP assertion that SAPs were helping Africa to achieve macro-economic stability. It found that 'in many cases sustained economic growth has not materialized, the rate of investment rather than improve has tended to decrease, budget and balance of payments deficits have tended to widen after some temporary relief and debt service obligations have become unbearable'.[69] Worse (for the World Bank), AAF-SAP questioned the research methods and statistics used by the World Bank that informed its conclusion about the success of SAPs in Africa. The intellectual honesty of the Bank was being called into question.

AAF-SAP advocated a more comprehensive approach to development in Africa, for, in its view, as well as that of many other Africans and Africanists, SAPs dealt with the symptoms of the African crisis, not the root causes. Furthermore, SAPs continued the fallacy of the post-World War II paradigm in development thinking that economic growth equalled development. That, according to AAF-SAP, led the World Bank to overlook the social costs of adjustment, especially on the poor. AAF-SAP's critique amounted to a fusillade from a double-barrelled gun: not only was Africa not returning on a path to prosperity thanks to SAPs, it was actually regressing, because of the enormous social costs of SAPs on the poor.

AAF-SAP advocated a number of policies that were anathema to the World Bank. It stressed the reinvigoration of the food-producing sector, as well as the cash crop sector. The aim of this was to make Africa more self-reliant in food production. AAF-SAP supported African industrialization, but one linked to the continent's primary sector (agriculture). AAF-SAP saw SAPs' emphasis on cash crop exports as shortsighted and limiting. An industrialization strategy that was based on using Africa's raw materials as inputs would allow for the capture of the value added benefits by African countries; in addition, it would reduce the enclave nature of African economies, wherein a small industrial sector, usually controlled by comprador elements and multinational corpora-tions (MNCs) operates independently from the other sectors (agriculture and services). Above all, AAF-SAP called for a development that was human-centred, for development, at the end of day, was about people, not dry statistical indices pointing upward. In this connection, AAF-SAP called for structural adjustment programs that actually improved the lives of the poor, or at least spared them of further misery. In sum, AAF-SAP advocated transformation rather than adjustment.[70] In addition, AAF-SAP was a philosophical affirmation that Africans knew best how to solve Africa's problems.

However, two things must be said about AAF-SAP. Firstly, it was not the first critique of SAPs and, by association, the Berg Report. African intellectuals had studied both and publicized their nefariousness independently of AAF-SAP. Some of their works are cited in this study (e.g., Onimode 1989; Olukoshi 1989; Ndegwa 1985, etc.). Nor was AAF-SAP the only time Africans had tried to develop African-inspired solutions to the continent's problems. The last major effort in this direction was the OAU-sponsored Lagos Plan of Action (LAP), which, like AAF-SAP, had called for greater African self-reliance, especially in food production and other essentials of life, and preceded the Berg Report at least by one full year.

I shall not say much about LAP, for the focus of this part of the work is ultimately on Bank lending policy history, but that LAP came before the Berg Report is very significant. It means, once again, that Africans in the early 1980s were seriously attempting to address Africa's woes well before they became a cause célèbre in the 'donor' community. But why African ministers of finance, who also act, on paper, as governors of the World Bank, felt it necessary to request that the Bank undertake a study of Africa's development crisis (hence the Berg Report), when they had one (LAP) produced by their own organization (OAU) underscores the dependency of African countries vis-à-vis the international financial institutions (IFIs) and the West in general. For, in spite of its stated goal of moving Africa toward self-reliance, LAP itself expected 'donors' to finance at least one third of its budget.

Secondly, and this is rather unfortunate, in spite of the publicity it received, AAF-SAP, like LAP, had little effect on Bank policy behaviour. Structural Adjustment Programs remained at the heart of Bank lending policy in sub-Saharan Africa throughout the 1990s. However, AAF-SAP may have forced a change in Bank rhetoric. In *From Crisis to Sustainable Growth,* the Bank 'strongly supports the call for a human-centred development strategy made by the ECA and UNICEF'.[71] The World Bank, once again, often does this: it seeks to remain above the fray, even if this means incorporating the views of its critics in its rhetoric while pursuing its own policies. Its posture toward alternative worldviews is to, first, reject, and if those persist, co-opt. The rhetorical demi-tours (not U-turns) of the Bank are facilitated by the passing of the baton from one Bank president to another. Each Bank president essentially tries to leave his mark on the organization. The recalibration of SAPs with a 'human face'[72] befell Barber Conable, the affable successor to the austere and market-oriented Clausen (a theory of Bank behaviour is offered in the next section).

By the end of the decade (1980s), the wisdom of neo-liberalism would seem to be confirmed by economic recovery in the United States and Britain and the impending collapse of Stalinist political economies in Eastern Europe in 1989 and soon thereafter (1991) the Soviet Union. But in Africa, two decades of SAPs have made conditions worse, not better, which leads to the easy conclusion that SAPs are more albatross than elixir.[73] For the Third World as a whole, the 1990s have been dubbed the 'lost decade', just as the 1980s were so designated for sub-Saharan Africa.[74] True, the percentage of people living on less than one dollar a day dropped from 30 percent to 23 percent in the 1990s, but much of the reason for the apparent gain is due to improvement in the economic per-formance of China and India, two of the world's most populous countries, and China's development efforts have been more dirigiste than laissez faire.[75] Overall, poverty continues unabated, HIV/AIDS is reducing life expectancy in scores of countries,[76] states are on the brink of collapse while others have seen their sovereignty eroded (thus making them proto-states), and the rich, taking advantage of increased opportunities for private accumulation in a globalized political economy, are getting richer.[77]

It was, perhaps, in partial recognition of the limited success of SAPs that the Bank adopted a 'kinder, gentler' approach in the 1990s. Current Bank president James Wolfensohn has worked hard to articulate this approach and dispel the notion that the Bank is blindly pro-free markets, viscerally anti-states and insensitive to poverty. In 1997 Wolfensohn stressed that: 'Far from supporting a minimalist approach to the state, development requires an effec-tive state, one that plays a catalytic, facilitating role, encouraging and complementing the activities of private business and individuals. Certainly, state-dominated development has failed. But so has stateless development—a message that comes through all too clearly in the agonies of people in collapsed states such as Liberia and Somalia.'[78]

On the surface, Wolfenshon's utterance is strong stuff. The rhetoric suggests that the Bank now recognizes the importance of states to sound economies, but nowhere in the aforementioned quote and in other Bank publications is it suggested that states should go beyond encouraging and complementing private sector activities. As it always has, the Bank discourages direct public ownership of productive assets, strong regulatory regimes and public goods delivery that cannot be potentially undertaken by private actors. In spite of rhetoric of building 'institutional capacity', the Bank has done little to rescue failed states or strengthen those that are in danger of failing. This task usually devolves to the United Nations, typically after much diplomatic wrangling and when it is too late, and humanitarian organizations. The 1980s were the decade of dismantling the 'meddlesome', interventionist, industrial asset-owning state; the 1990s were the decade of constructing the minimalist, pro-free-market state.

At the same time, the last decade of the 20th century also saw a return to the populist rhetoric of the 1970s about poverty reduction, while in the 1980s (the era of SAPs) Bank lending policy was couched much more in technocratic terms. In 1999 the World Bank (and IMF) launched the Poverty Reduction Strategy Papers (PRSPs) approach to poverty reduction, which may well have been the Bank's (and IMF's) answer to accusations of heavy handedness in lending. PRSPs are basically documents prepared by borrowing governments that are intended to demonstrate widespread participation by stakeholders (governments, entrepreneurs, non-governmental organizations, academics, etc) in the design of projects aimed at poverty reduction over several years for which external (e.g., Bank) support is to be sought.[79] Five principles are said to underpin the PRSP approach. PRSPs must be country-driven, meaning that countries should take collective ownership of PRSPs. For this to happen, there must be a spirit of partnership among all stakeholders: government, the private sector, civil society and donors. The Bank also stresses that PRSPs be result-oriented: they must show that their outcomes will benefit the poor. They should be comprehensive, thus underscoring the multidimensional character of poverty. Finally, PRSPs should have a long-term perspective, perhaps an oblique admission by the Bank, at long last, that it does not have an answer to poverty reduction.[80] The World Bank sees PRSPs as the means by which to bring together governments, civil society and donors to attain the UN's Millennium Development Goals, which include cutting world poverty in half by 2015.

As is customary with the World Bank, the rhetoric of PRSPs is so unassailable that it should elicit no objection. The policy reality of PRSPs, however, is different. According to Christian Aid, 'the World Bank and IMF have linked their financing to poverty reduction strategy papers (PRSPs). These are ostensibly a country's own plans to cut poverty, but they have also become gateways to loans and debt relief. In order to access the money they need, recipient countries have to fulfil a complex set of conditions.'[81] Interestingly, these are the same conditions that were routinely attached to structural adjustment lending and have nothing to do with poverty reduction (and indeed, if the experience of the 1980s is any guide, are likely to exacerbate poverty): trade liberalization, privatization of hitherto publicly provided services, cost recovery, etc. In sum, in spite of the lofty rhetoric, PRSPs are, in fact, a back door way of (re) imposing the conditionalities of the 1980s on borrowing countries, thus keeping them in the march toward a neo-liberal world economy. One should not be surprised if the Millennium Development Goals are not met in 2015, as they seem unlikely to be at the moment (2005).

The Bank underwent another (rhetorical) makeover in the last decade of the century that cannot be passed over, for it, too, fits a familiar pattern in Bank behaviour. Beginning in 1990, specifically in Benin, African countries began to liberalize their political system(s). This took many forms, of which national conferences, or calls for their occurrence, leading to multiparty elections (following the legalization of opposition parties) were the most common in Francophone Africa. Benin, Togo, Congo-Brazzaville, Congo, Gabon and Cameroon held these gatherings, with varying degrees of seriousness and success.

In virtually all African countries pressure for democratization came, in no small part, from groups that had been hurt by SAPs and 'the anthropology of anger' created by government mismanagement, repression and lies.[82] Among other things, these groups wanted an end to spiralling prices for basic services, such as health care, education and everyday utilities (water, electricity, etc.). Recent college graduates also wanted jobs, many eliminated by the SAPs imposed on African governments, which mandated retrenchment in the size of the civil service. In other words, pro-democracy forces in Africa were fighting as much for social democracy as they were for the imprimaturs of liberal democracy (legalization of opposition parties, free and fair elections, political freedoms, etc.), however important these were. This period of great political effervescence has evoked comparisons with Prague Spring and revolutionary France.[83] Nevertheless, in spite of the social democratic character of Africa's second political revolution (the first being the fight for decolonization), or perhaps because of it, the Bank saw an opening for co-optation.

Before 1990 one would be hard pressed to find any Bank publication in which the words democracy and good governance were mentioned, except as an afterthought. Indeed, until then the attitude of the World Bank toward democracy could be characterized as either indifferent or hostile. The Bank often claimed it did not meddle in politics, and that its activities in borrowing countries were of a technical (read: apolitical) nature; the same applied to the IMF. There was even latent hostility toward democracy, inasmuch as the prevailing view in the 1960s and 1970s, expounded most strongly by Samuel Huntington, was that what the Third World needed were governments strong enough to maintain order, not democracy.[84] Democracy in developing countries was likely to cause rising expectations among newly empowered groups, which could create frustration as such expectations were unlikely to be met. This, in turn, was a recipe for de-legitimacy and instability, and unstable regimes could not implement difficult macro-economic policies and negotiate the financing of complex projects in the face of popular opposition. Organizations like the World Bank acquiesced in the emasculation of formal opposition and the spread of one-party states throughout Africa, on the (false) premise that democracy, even in its limited, liberal form, was too messy and potentially destabilizing to countries that needed, first and foremost, development.[85]

After 1990 there was an about-face. The Bank began to emphasize good governance, which it conflated with democracy, and eventually this would become one item on the laundry list of conditionalities associated with SAPs, although good governance would never enjoy the same cachet as the other items (discussed earlier). Indeed, as Part III suggests, where Bank lending is concerned, there is no democracy bonus: countries that have democratized (i.e., 'free' according to Freedom House ranking) are no more likely to be the recipient of Bank lending than those that have not ('less free'). What then explains the adjustment (pun intended) in Bank rhetoric?

Firstly, as a concept democracy connotes such positive values that it is virtually impossible for any respectable person (or institution) to actively oppose it. Democracy may be de-prioritized as a goal of government, in favour of, say, 'development', but not rejected outright, which explains why the most repressive of countries have found it necessary to add democratic to their official name. Secondly, in the context of sub-Saharan Africa in the early 1990s democracy, as a political reality in the making, had seemed such an unstoppable force that it was definitely easier, even for those who had helped to undermine it, to join the bandwagon and from within divert its trajectory. Finally, from the Bank's point of view, liberal democracy could be useful, inasmuch as democratically elected governments could help legitimize SAPs in a way that Bank promises of economic recovery never could — hence the emphasis in country after country in Africa on elections as sui generis evidence of transition to democratic rule.[86] In rural Africa, in particular, multiparty elections have been known to favour well-financed candidates and parties backed by foreign interests; they tend to create either new patronage networks or reinforce old ones. Thus, multiparty elections in sub-Saharan Africa posed no great threat to continuity in economic policy; incumbents and challengers were expected to sing from the same page book of SAPs, no matter who won.[87] The Bank, therefore, was taking no risk by seeming to support democracy, even though, once again, such a support was often more rhetorical than a harbinger of real change in policy.

Conclusion

Part I has shown that throughout its history the World Bank has been committed to a (neo-liberal) vision of the Third World, with Bank lending and the conditionalities attached thereto in the 1980s and 1990s as the primary vehicle for implementing that vision. It has also shown that the World Bank does not operate in a vacuum; the Bank is a visible international financial institution (IFI) that deals with sovereign governments under the glare of friends and foes alike. Thus, the World Bank has had to jettison its position periodically, to co-opt worldviews that are contrary to its own, for the purpose of seeming to accommodate critics. It is safe to state that, in its nearly 60-year history, the Bank has often shifted rhetoric, occasionally changed the reality of policy but never ideology. In the new millennium the Bank (re)defines its mission as poverty reduction when the very policies pursued by the Bank (SAPs) in the last two decades have, in fact, helped to increase poverty in Africa. The dissonance raises at least one question: How can the gap between Bank rhetoric and practice be theoretically explained? The reader is urged to read the next section.

Part II

Theory Building and the World Bank

With thousands of employees scattered around the world, annual lending in the tens of billions USD and 'shareholders' that are countries rather than individual investors, the World Bank is a large, complex organization. Furthermore, the Bank's task is complex: promoting a neo-liberal economic order that causes havoc on the world's poor while pretending to pursue poverty reduction worldwide through 'development'. The Bank's problem is simply this: how to achieve market penetration of Third World economies in the name of economic growth and development, while market-oriented policies typically result in exactly the opposite of what is explicitly stated or intended and are often resisted by the very elites (and populace) whose support is needed for their implementation.

Any serious study of the World Bank has got to start with this reality, that is, the bureaucratic and task complexity of the World Bank. Simple theorizing will not do; one does not analyze the World Bank the way neoclassical microeconomic theory treats the firm. A better perspective, I believe, is provided by organization theory, in particular, systems theory. But even this can only offer partial explanation of the disconnect between Bank rhetoric and lending policy behaviour, for systems theory does not address the dynamic processes that go on inside organizations; its thrust, as I will argue later, is how organizations adapt and adjust to the external environment in order to survive.

A complete theory of the World Bank would have to take into account how the structure of the organization, divided as it is among various divisions or units; headquarters, regional and in-country missions; specialists from various academic disciplines (although neo-liberal economists are probably overrepresented in the lot) and a board of executives directors, whose membership is comprised of representatives from various countries, creates cleavages that can potentially be consequential for policy or at least cannot be ignored by the leadership of the Bank. In this connection, the bureaucratic politics model developed by Graham T. Allison and Morton Halperin to explain the handling of the Cuban Missile Crisis, although somewhat dated and seemingly unrelated to the topic at hand, may be a basis for understanding Bank behaviour.

Finally, if one assumes, not unreasonably, that the World Bank's primary concern is to survive as an organization and not be put out of business, and if one further assumes that the professionals who work at the Bank are concerned, first and foremost, about advancing their career, either within the Bank or in the (under)development industry, rational choice theory may then prove very useful in explaining Bank lending policy and rhetoric. Thus, the approach that I take here shall include macro-level theorizing (systems theory), intermediary level theorizing (bureaucratic politics) and, to a much lesser extent, micro-level theorizing (rational choice).

I argue that the World Bank is an open systems organization that often behaves as though it were a closed, or rational, system one. Even when it is at its best, the Bank must jettison the requirements of a closed system with those of an open systems organization — not an easy act. Three questions immediately arise: what is a system, what makes the Bank an open, as opposed to a closed, system, and why does the Bank not always behave the way it should (i.e., as an open systems organization)?

A system is an assemblage of parts, which are meant to work together toward the achievement of a common goal. A system is thus characterized by complexity, interdependency and purpose. Modern organizations are social systems, according to March and Simon:

> Organizations are assemblages of interacting human beings and they are the largest assemblages in our society that have anything resembling a central coordinative system...The high specificity of structure and coordination within organizations — as contrasted with the diffuse and variable relations among organizations and among unorganized individuals — marks off the individual organization as a sociological unit comparable in significance to the individual organism in biology.[88]

Not all systems are the same; some are closed, or rational, while others are open. Rationality here means technical rationality, that is to say, in the case of organizations, that 'a series of actions is organized in such a way as to lead to predetermined goals with maximum efficiency.'[89] In other words, in the closed system organization knowledge is complete, and, more broadly, the means are internally available to accomplish the ends. The closed system organization is self-propelling and needs little external support; it is, in other words, a machine.[90] Closed system theorists are concerned mainly with internal design. Decisions in this type of organization flow from top to bottom; they are specific directives (or commands) from super-ordinates (management) to sub-ordinates (workers), which the latter 'merely' need to follow to the letter. Closed system organizations do not dismiss the external environment entirely, nor, however, do they assume that are they dependent upon it for survival.

By contrast, an open system is 'capable of self-maintenance based on a throughput of resources from its environment, such as a living cell.'[91] An open system organization cannot survive without the external environment, which it uses to garner the 'ingredients' it needs for survival. These may include financial resources, intelligence (in other words, information) and political support. Implicit in the open systems model is that the organization is not an isolated entity; it is part of a larger system (i.e., society or, in the case of the World Bank, international society) upon which it feeds and which it must feed. Here organization should be designed with the environment in mind.[92] A major, somewhat contradictory, goal of the open systems organization is boundary maintenance or buffering (so it can fulfil the tasks for which it was designed) and boundary spanning (so it can take on new tasks and acquire what it needs from the external environment to perform existing tasks and ultimately survive).

The World Bank is objectively an open systems organization. It cannot survive without the external environment, which it depends on for financing, staffing, political support, or at least tolerance, and task assignment. Furthermore, the external environment of the World Bank, as stated earlier, is complex. It includes borrowing governments, donor governments (those that contribute to the replenishment of IDA), other multilateral development institutions (IMF, UN, WTO, regional development banks), Non-Governmental Organizations (NGOs), universities, etc. The reality of the open systems nature of the World Bank means that it cannot really ignore the external environment, or seems to do so. This explains the rhetorical behaviour of the Bank, which is subject to change as external pressures come and go. Subjectively, reflexively and programmatically, however, the Bank tends to behave more like a closed system, or rational, organization, because of the ideology of development.[93] This explains its policy behaviour, which is more stable and consistent but not necessarily rigid or totally impervious to change. The dissonance between rhetoric and policy, I contend, explains much of the Bank's malfunction.

It will be recalled that in the closed system organization there is a presumption of a connection between means and ends and that both are known. Furthermore, relations between super-ordinates and sub-ordinates involve commands from the former, which the latter are expected to faithfully execute. Closed system organizations pay great attention to organizational design. The organization here is a machine, whose parts can be made to work perfectly so as to achieve optimality in performance (measured in terms of effectiveness and, especially, efficiency). The World Bank very much sees development in this way, namely: (a) it knows what development is and (b) it knows how to bring development about. All Third World countries have to do is listen and implement. If they do, they are 'rewarded' with Bank funding (the way scientific management advocated higher wages to motivate workers at the turn of the 20th century). And what happens when countries do not develop after following Bank advice? It must be they were not really listening!

The entire history of the Bank suggests a mechanistic approach bordering on hubris. Development is presented as the inevitable end-result of following the 'right' policies, which almost invariably are biased toward markets. In the 1950s the trick was to invest in power plants, steel plants and roads (a direct outgrowth of the reconstruction efforts in Western Europe and Japan after World War II). In the 1960s and 1970s, the emphasis was on technology transfer, easy lending and some investment in agriculture. The 1980s and 1990s brought Getting Prices Right (a throwback from the 1970s) and policy-based lending (SAPs). Each time, once again, policies are (re)presented with the certainty of astronomical movements that cannot fail. Yet neither development as an end nor the means to achieve it connotes the universality in agreement that is presumed to exist for both.

What is development? In its epistemology, development is a biological concept attesting to changes (typically growth) in a living organism (such as a cell). Transposed to the social realm, development becomes a metaphor, and metaphors never help to completely explain reality, only to make sense of it with the use of imageries from other domains. In the West development is generally understood to mean (falsely) economic growth, which will translate (again falsely) into material prosperity for all; however, different cultural meanings attend the concept in other parts of the world. In fact, early Christianity, the one leg upon which western civilization stands (the other being Judaism), had a very different notion of what it means to be 'rich', and Jesus Christ himself did not hold out much hope that the materially rich could enter his kingdom in large numbers (he bet, instead, on the ability of a camel to squeeze through the eye of a needle).

Even if it is agreed that development essentially entails increased wealth, and with that freedom from basic wants, as Amartya Sen suggests,[94] there is probably less agreement on the means to bring it about. Does anyone really know what causes poverty, much less how to reduce it? In circumstances where there is agreement on goals but disagreement on means, policy must necessarily be the result 'informed judgment'. For problems that occasion agreement on ends but disagreement on means, according to Thompson and Tuden, suggest that there is 'lack of acceptable proof of the merits of alternatives'.[95] In such cases, since alternatives cannot be objectively weighed for their efficacy, then decisions should be based on majority rule. In the context of development in the Third World, the World Bank has shown that it knows no more about development than the countries that use its funds. A sensible approach would be to let these countries take the lead in designing their own programs; this, at least, would be democratic. In circumstances such as the one depicted in this paragraph (where there may be agreement on ends but disagreements on means) policy must also be experimental, inasmuch as decision makers do not really know what will work a priori. The paucity of knowledge must give way to pragmatism, the latter unimpeded by ideology or dogma. And the most appropriate organization for this task environment is the flexible, open systems, organization.

For the World Bank, however, experimental policy-making poses serious problems. Such an approach entails that failure is a possibility, because knowledge is incomplete — i.e., knowledge about the task itself and the means for its accomplishment. But, as I have tried to show, from the beginning in the woods of chilly New Hampshire development was put in the same imaginaire as reconstruction. President Harry Truman's 'Four Points' speech did not leave any doubt that the West, led by the US, knew what development was and how to bring it to the Third World. Development meant building industrial plants, huge dams for electricity generation and roads. After all, these were the activities for which the Bank's services were retained after World War II, which it delivered with some success in Europe. The US, with its money and know-how, would now lead the way in the Third World to eradicate diseases, fight poverty, etc. The only note of caution was this: at Bretton Woods, the partici-pants were reluctant to continue the practice, common before World War II in Latin America, of government-to-government lending. It was thought that this approach was responsible for the 'gun-boat' diplomacy of that era, wherein creditor countries felt that they had no choice but to threaten, and in some cases occupy, borrowing countries on the verge of bankruptcy or civil war, in order to safeguard and recoup their 'investment' (Haiti, Dominican Republic, Nicaragua, etc.).

By creating a lending institution, in which all governments were nominal owners while real ownership was in the hands of the advanced industrial countries (especially the US), with everyday operation devolved to technocrats, the founders felt that future imperialist wars could be avoided. Borrowing countries were more apt to listen to the advice of ostensibly apolitical specialists well-versed in economic 'science' and backed by the threat of sanctions (i.e., denial of access to Bank funds). Furthermore, in a world in which international relations were about to become bi-polar, the US was loath to give its adversary, the former Soviet Union, any ammunition, any chance to gain greater influence. Pro-US allies in the Third World could be found more easily if, rather than being occupied militarily, promises of development 'aid' were made to them, provided that, in return, their economic policies, diplomacy, but not necessarily political system (this would come much later, i.e., after 1990), were consonant with those of the West. To show the Third World how to develop, the US was even willing to dispatch its experts and modernization theorists and give its blessing to new multilateral institutions. In the new dispensation of the post-War the World Bank (and IMF) would become major players in the development discourse and North-South relations.

The (con)fusion of reconstruction with development means that the World Bank must pretend it knows what development is and how to bring it about, lest it stands to lose not only credibility but even raison d'être. After all, the West looks to the Bank to solve the problems of the 'rest'. How would it look if Bank officials threw up their hands, in recognition that development is not a sure thing and that they do not have all the answers to poverty reduction? Such an admission might indeed be a first in the history of modern organizations and would be heroic; but it would probably spell the death of the World Bank as we know it. The Bank's demise would no doubt be welcome in many quarters around the world but not inside its walls. Organizations seek to survive, not die by their own hands. Where would the Bank be if poverty were really eliminated?

From the beginning the Bank also presumed that it had the means to bring about development, and these were essentially market-based, except for public utilities, which too would fall prey to privatization in the 1980s. The World Bank's bias toward markets or private interests stems from two sources, one organizational and the other ideological. In the pursuit of internal economy (i.e., efficiency) organizations have a tendency to develop standard operating procedures in response to tasks with which they are familiar, and when new tasks arise, rather than developing new procedures, they tend to construe them as old ones, thereby maintaining business as usual. Overtime, these procedures may become so embedded in the organization's culture that they are practically impossible to uproot, unless, that is, cataclysmic events occur, charismatic leaders emerge, or both. Beyond the rigidity of their operating methods, bureaucratic organizations, in order to survive, also tend to take on tasks for which they are maladapted.

Stiglitz (cited earlier) reported how development was added to the Bank's official name — the International Bank for Reconstruction and Development — 'almost as an afterthought' when it should have been separately and carefully calibrated. To rebuild is not develop: the former entails (re)erecting that which previously existed, and therefore that with which people are familiar, the latter connotes creation, newness, unfamiliarity, uncertainty. In the aftermath of World War II there should have been an International Bank for Development tout court, perhaps with some connection to the various regional development banks that sprang in the post-war era.

These regional Banks — i.e., the African Development Bank, the Asian Development Bank and the Inter-American Development Bank — whose record in fostering development, alas, is not much better than that of the World Bank, could have exhibited the kind of flexibility and willingness to experiment that the development process requires. Thus, instead of lending strictly to national governments, they could have lent to regional ones and non-state actors (e.g., peasant cooperatives, for-profit firms, etc.). They also could have been designed to be under popular control, thus fostering economic democracy (how many Africans own shares of the ADB?). Last but not least, they could have acted as gatekeepers to Third World currency markets, thereby protecting their economies from predation by currency traders.

The World Bank's preference for markets as the means to bring about development is also guided by ideology. This is a critique of Bank policy behaviour that is common among students of the institution. I have delayed discussing ideology in Part II until now, because I wanted to bring a fresh (i.e., organization theory) perspective to the debate on the World Bank. However, there is no question that it plays a major part in the modus operandi of the Bank (as I tried to show in Part I). Ideology is hereby defined as 'an economizing device by which individuals [and organizations] come to terms with their environment and are provided with a 'worldview' so that the decision-making process is simplified.'[96] The World Bank's worldview is that of the neo-classical economic theorist for whom seemingly voluntary transactions, or markets, are the best means of resource allocation. It is committed to a world economy free of government control, or with as little of it as possible. The syllogism underlying this commitment is simple: because they are superior to hierarchies in allocating resources, markets drive economic growth, which is a condition for development, therefore, development, more or less, requires markets.[97] One cannot understand Bank policy without understanding this postulate; neo-classical economic ideology thus underpins Bank policy.

However, it is worth noting that the centrality of the choice-theoretic approach embedded in neo-classical economics does not confine the Bank to an asphyxiating straightjacket, for the free market ideology which has arisen from the neo-classical model, as North points out, 'has not developed within a comprehensive framework of social, political, and philosophical (not to mention metaphysical) theory.'[98] The world of the neo-classical economic theorist is much more limited; basically, it is a world of what ifs: what if there were multiple buyers and sellers, what if information were perfect and could be costlessly obtained, what if there were no barriers to market entry and exit? Knowing these conditions seldom obtain in the real world, neo-classical economists are often willing to settle for less, until such time as they may obtain more (i.e., move to the pure market model).

Furthermore, neo-classical economic theory and its handmaiden (neo-liberalism), even in its moment of triumph (from the 1980s onward) is far from a consensus, even among mainstream economists. In order words, precisely because it is incomplete as a worldview (certainly not as complete as Marxism), neo-classical economic theory has shown surprising resilience, even in the face of overwhelming evidence to the contrary. And precisely because neo-classical economic theory has always been contested, real world practitioners have had to make grudging concessions to critics. Perhaps no international agency has been more successful than the World Bank in jettisoning free market ideology to fit the political (and other) realities of the moment.

Contrary to popular notions, ideology is not always dogma; it is sometimes — indeed often — malleable at the margins, capable, as it were, of accommodating challenges. Any ideology, if it is to survive in an ever-changing environment, is open to mutations while preserving its core essence. When ideology becomes dogma, inflexibility obtains. At any given time, an ideology may be confronted with certain socio-political, economic and other imperatives (realities), which limit the purity of its application.[99] Unless it is able to co-opt these imperatives, or develop stronger counter imperatives in maintenance of the status quo, the ideology may even die.

The World Bank is, without question, the night watchman of neo-liberalism in our time, but, at the same time, has shown incomparable dexterity in the exercise of this function. Neo-liberal ideology provides the overall parameter to Bank action, but within that a number of factors may influence Bank policy in the immediate term including geo-politics, the resource base of countries and their size, Bank presidents, Bank fund-raising methods, popular pressure and, as I argue below, bureaucratic politics inside the Bank. Thus it is not enough to identify neo-liberalism as the only basis for Bank action; such an approach reduces ideology to an idée fixe that does not take into account the complex and dynamic world in which the Bank operates. It cannot explain, for example, why the World Bank invested heavily in agriculture and in the poor in the 1970s and supported, at least rhetorically, democracy in the 1990s after decades of foreswearing politics. It cannot explain why the World Bank has taken on debt relief as its new mantra and now supports (again rhetorically) strengthening the state,[100] after years of ignoring debt as a factor in the African crisis and reducing the state to its simplest expression, in spite of repeated warnings from African scholars and Africanists (Olukoshi and Olusanya 1989; Onimode 1992; Olukoshi and Laako 1996; Simon, Spengen, Dixon and Narman 1995). In sum, a non-nuanced focus on ideology adduces inflexibility to an institution that is simply betrayed by the record of the last 60 years. I have underscored the Bank's ability to adapt throughout this study, not only in rhetoric but also in policy. The World Bank has been consistent but not rigid or dogmatic; it has shown stability in its commitment to a particular worldview, or ideology, but its policies, and especially rhetoric, have been malleable enough to make for organizational survival in a turbulent environment. This is why Part II has sought to put ideology in an organizational context, rather than viewing it as all-determining.

The World Bank, as stated earlier, has thousands of employees scattered throughout the world (to be exact: 9,300), a board of governors composed of representatives from every member country (184), a board of 24 executive governors, scores of bureaux responsible for every minutia of Bank activities and a multi-billion lending budget. In addition, World Bank presidents are among the most visible public figures in the World. Any theory of the World Bank would have to consider bureaucratic politics as a factor in Bank lending policy behaviour. Here I must concede that the model I am about to present is not actually descriptive of the Bank. Rather, it is a way, perhaps a new way, of getting readers to think about the World Bank and, for the ambitious and courageous ones, undertake research in this direction. At the end of the day, a theory need not be descriptive of reality; it only needs to provide a logical explanation of its occurrence, which then should be tested for validation or rejection.[101] Here goes.[102]

Firstly, given the size of the bank, the complexity of its tasks, as well as that of its environment, it is safe to posit that what passes for Bank 'policy', be it in lending or anywhere else, is not the work of some super-ordinate policy maker, such as Bank presidents, but rather the composite result of the preferences of various Bank officials (henceforth to be referred to as players), including obviously Bank presidents but also the directors of specialized units (e.g., the economic analysis unit), members of the board of executive directors, who technically oversee the Bank's daily operations, regional directors and even in-country resident directors.[103] If the above is true, as I suspect it is, then intra-bureaucratic politics is an important factor to consider when analyzing Bank lending and the conditionalities attached thereto (henceforth to be referred as the game); after all, lending money is the most important activity in which the Bank is engaged on a daily basis. One would expect every important player to want to take part in the game. This may have been especially true since the early 1980s, when lending became the instrument by which the World Bank has sought to influence (some would say control) the macro-economic policies of borrowing countries.

Secondly, given that some of the rules of the game have contradictory effects (viz. devaluation stimulates exports but it is also inflationary, as it makes imported goods more expensive; cost recovery may lead to an increase in the supply of government services but may also price the poor out of the 'market' for such services), one would expect a good deal of bargaining among players as to what rules should or should not be included in the game. Thus, Bank lending policy and the concomitant conditionalities are made 'not by a single rational choice, but by pulling and hauling'.[104] What players are interested in are the outcomes of the game, not in regards to the effects that Bank policy has on borrowing countries, although it would be too cynical to conjecture that no one inside the Bank cares about the Third World, but outcomes in regard to the content of policy. Simply put, players are interested in whether their preferences are included in the package of conditionalities that are attached to Bank lending.

A bureaucratic theory of the World Bank would have to pay attention to incentives. In the schemata being sketched here the incentives are at least two-fold: players may feel so strongly about a rule that, from their point of view, it has to be part of the game (monetarists, for example, may feel that a tight monetary policy must be included in adjustment lending while free traders may prefer to focus on lifting trade restrictions); furthermore, they may feel that playing is the only way to advance their career within the bank and enhance their reputation in the larger community. Players may also have an incentive to play not because of the gains they expect to accrue to them personally but to their divisions or units. Hence, as Allison and Hallerin put it, where players stand on a policy issue depends on where they sit.

On the other hand, one would also expect players to limit the number of their colleagues eligible to play, unless they thought that enlargement would be of benefit to them. The rational choice notion of winning coalitions is useful here: players may reach out to other players outside of their bureaux (or constituents) to create alliances to strengthen their position. In particularly important games, top players would insist that they take the field, relegating lesser players to the bench. Also, top players need not be formally associated with the World Bank. Players might also include high-level officials within the US Department of the Treasury. It is not even far-fetched to conjecture that dissident players inside the Bank might sometimes encourage players in borrowing governments to stand firm in defence of policies that they support but that the Bank as an institution does not. I am suggesting here that uniformity inside the Bank is not a foregone conclusion or static; rather, it may be conditional or situational and dynamic.

Finally, Bank lending policy may be assumed to follow action channels, that is to say, the regularized sets of procedures that are intended to produce Bank actions, which are defined as the various acts by the Bank that can be perceived by outsiders as representative of the organization's official policies. Where lending to individual countries is concerned, the in-country resident of the World Bank and its regional director usually play an important role, as do the site visit teams that are dispatched by headquarters to negotiate with a prospective borrower. Major Bank actions of the type theorized in this section typically involve the production of a report by a well-known expert, or team of experts (the Berg Report), or a public address of the president of the World, either at the annual meeting of the Board of Governors (McNamara in Nairobi in 1974) or during the passing of the baton from one outgoing president of the Bank to an incoming one (Clausen in 1981). In sum, policy decisions are not made on whim, nor are they made by a single individual.

The question is, given the multiciplicity of actors and channels that are probably involved in its decision making, how is it that that the World Bank has managed to make policies at all, and how is it that these have been fairly consistent (i.e., pro- free markets or neo-liberal) over a long period of time? And what explains the policies that, on the surface at least, appear to deviate from the norm?

Propositions

a) Even though the World Bank has many sub-systems (i.e., multiple units with specialized functions), the number of players involved in Bank games expands or contracts, depending on the nature of the games being played. The bigger the game, i.e., the more important the policy being considered, the higher the calibre of the players, meaning that decisions that signal important shifts in lending and priorities by the Bank will likely involve a limited number of top officials, even though the action channels that produce such decisions may initially include a large number of sub-ordinates. The following super-ordinates participate in Bank games, especially big ones: Bank presidents, members of the executive directors board, especially those from the countries with the largest number of shares (i.e., US, France, Japan, Germany and the UK), top officials within the specialized units (e.g., the economic analysis unit) and regional directors. Decision making here is facilitated by the small number of players who actually play.

b) Consistency in Bank policy is explained not only by ideology but also by the fact that Bank presidents have the power to appoint top officials to various units, including the economic research unit. In fact, Bank presidents have used their appointees to this unit to signal important shifts in Bank lending orientation. Thus, consistency in Bank games stems from the fact that top players are generally on the same team. Furthermore, one Bank president (McNamara) served for nearly 13 years and the outgoing president has served for 10 years. Thus in its 60-year history two Bank presidents have accounted for over 1/3 of the institution's existence. That's consistency in personnel at the highest level, which begets consistency in policy.

c) Ceteris paribus, policy shifts will occur at the Bank when there is a changing of the guard from one Bank president to another, which also results in personnel changes in the important bureaux or units.

d) Official, generally populist, rhetoric, by the Bank that contradicts reality (policy) is intended not only to silence opposition from the external environment but also neutralize that of players left on the sidelines. In other words, Bank rhetoric is aimed as much at mitigating the effects of bureaucratic politics as it does extra-bureaucratic politics.

e) Populist policies that appear to contradict Bank ideological discourse are likely to be embraced if support for them 'bubble up' from within the Bank and from without (i.e., the external environment of borrowing governments, other multilateral lenders, donor governments, social activists, progressive academics and think tanks, etc.). External pressure and the in-country residents and regional experts of the Bank, especially in Africa, played an important role in the relatively enlightened policies of the 1970s, which were then embraced by McNamara.

f) Bank presidents are definitely players but they are also referees (were it not for the imagery presented earlier, which requires consistency in terminologies, brokers might be a better term). They play, mediate between players within the Bank and monitor (and sometimes listen to) the audience (the external environment).

Other Policy-Influencing Factors

An important aspect of Bank operations that has not received sufficient attention from students has to do with Bank capital formation. Yet it is absolutely essential for understanding how the external environment affects Bank policy. The World Bank, IBRD in particular, raises some of its money in capital markets through the issuance of bonds (valued at $19 billion in 2003), which are purchased by both individual and institutional investors mainly in the wealthy countries, and interest payments on existing loans. This modus operandi has enormous implications for the Bank's oft-stated objective, which is to reduce poverty worldwide. The value of existing Bank bonds, as well as the Bank's ability to issue such securities in the future, depend on the return on investment of projects funded by the Bank. Bank bonds typically have AAA status, the highest possible rating, as Bank literature proudly proclaims.[105]

Were the Bank to be seen to fund projects with low return on investment, or lend to countries that do not make at least interest payments on their debt, its bonds would probably be downgraded, and with it its ability to raise capital. This may well explain why even the poorest of countries are made to pay off their arrears to the Bank, before they are eligible for new Bank loans.[106] There is almost a built-in incentive for the Bank to fund some projects, but not others, and to lend money to some countries, but not others. Fundable projects will tend to be those with high visibility, large economies of scale, and sizable return on investment, in other words, gargantuanism; they will also tend to be projects that make heavy use of local (natural) resources. These characteristics favour middle-income countries well endowed in natural resources with relatively stable and technically competent government, as well as brick-and-mortar projects (as confirmed by our data). But the Bank is also officially committed to poverty reduction. This cannot be achieved, unless the Bank lends to poor countries, which have different needs, and where the return on investment may prove problematic for the value of Bank bonds.[107] The only way for the Bank to lend to poor countries and maintain its AAA bond rating is by insisting that the latter maintain fiscal discipline and not fall behind in servicing their debt. This may well explain why attempts at debt cancellation have thus far gone nowhere, for as long as countries are servicing their debt, or, more accurately, made to do so, the Bank, which has never lost money in its history, remains in the black and attractive to investors.

At the same time, the buyers of Bank securities, as stated earlier, include institutional investors who manage the funds of individuals and (or) collective entities (e.g., pension funds). In recent years, some indirect investors have taken an active role in influencing where their funds go. For example, in the 1980s pension fund managers for state and local governments in the U.S., under public pressure, were forced to divest in South Africa (e.g., Michigan State University). As far as I know, this tactic has not been employed to the World Bank, as perhaps it should be, but my point is a more general one: Because of the way it raises some of its capital, the World Bank is not immune from public pressure, and hence political struggles.[108]

If the Bank does not want to be seen to fund projects with low return on investment, neither does it want to be seen to support those that defile the environment, make the poor poorer and cause states to collapse, even if its lending policy results in precisely these outcomes. For the Bank maintaining a good public image — or at least steering clear of controversies — is also tied to capital formation. It is not an improbable conjecture that Bank rhetoric about poverty reduction is based in part on this reality. The Bank has to pay attention to the external environment, even while it pretends it has all the answers and has no programmatic need for outside input.

The World Bank is also funded by contributions from individual countries. The United States, European Union countries, such as Germany, France and Britain, and Japan are the Bank's largest contributors. These shareholders have an important voice in how the Bank is run and by whom. As the largest contributor to the World Bank, the United States has had a strong influence on the organization. U.S. officials can apply pressure on the Bank to deny or avail Bank funding to countries, and the decision as to which countries receive Bank support does not always depend on their needs, in spite of official Bank commitment to poverty reduction. The politicization of the World Bank has long been recognized by students of the institution.[109] Countries that need Bank assistance do not always get it, while others, provided they are well connected to important Bank shareholders (e.g., the United States and France), often receive generous loan packages.

Haiti was unable to borrow from the Bank from 1997 to 2004, in large part because of pressure from the United States, which was at loggerheads with the Lavalas (Flood) government of Jean-Bertrand Aristide over election results. But Egypt and Jordan, hardly democracies, not as poor as Haiti, but key allies of the United States in the Middle East, have received funding. Cameroon was able to keep World Bank (and IMF) aid flowing in the 1990s, because of support for the regime of President Paul Biya by France, although this came at a price that Paris initially resisted — i.e., the drastic devaluation of the CFA Franc in 1994, which sent the Cameroonian middle class reeling. Any serious analysis of Bank policy has to take into account the relative weight of countries in the international system, whether weight is measured in economic, demographic (i.e., population), geo-strategic and, yes, nuclear terms.

The World Bank is not always able to buffer itself against an 'intrusive' external environment. Chalmers Johnson may not be exaggerating when he calls the World Bank the informal arm of the U.S. Department of the Treasury.[110] But the United States is not always able to impose its will on countries through the Bank, and perhaps not even always on the Bank itself. As I have tried to show in this study, it matters who heads the World Bank. For Bank orientation is strongly shaped by Bank presidents. Robert McNamara, for example, was able to sell poverty reduction through rural development as the core mission of the World Bank. The Bank invested billions in the rural sector in the 1970s, although the logic underlying the effort, flawed as it was, did not alleviate poverty in the Third World.[111] Likewise, McNamara's successors — A.W. Clausen, Barber Conable, Lewis Preston and James Wolfensohn — brought different orientations to the Bank, shaped, no doubt, by their personal background and the changed international environment of the 1980s (i.e., the rise of neo-liberal ideology, the collapse of Marxist-Leninist regimes and ideology in Eastern Europe and the former Soviet Union, etc.).

In addition to the main contributors, the Bank of course deals with borrowing countries. This, too, is part of the external environment that informs Bank policy. State elites from borrowing countries have their own agendas, which may conflict with the Bank's. These may include limiting foreign control of strategic sectors of their economy, maintaining currency boards (to protect their currency from predation by international currency traders) and keeping food prices and those of essentials low through government subsidies, all of which are anathema to Bank neo-liberal efforts. Above all, state elites from borrowing countries are concerned about their own survival. In their calculus they have to weigh the potential costs (in social, economic and political terms) of erasing certain nationalist items from their policy agendas versus the benefits of receiving the next tranche of a Bank Stand-By Loan.

The orthodoxy of Bank (neo-liberal) policy toward borrowing countries depends on their size, the intensity of their needs, the availability of alternative sources of borrowing and the willingness of state elites to embrace (or reject) Bank strictures, among other factors. Russia was able to defy the World Bank and the IMF in the 1990s in a way that Bangladesh probably could not, and billions borrowed to support the falling rubble 'evaporated' practically overnight. Nevertheless, the collapse of Russia was deemed unthinkable in terms of the impact it would have on the world economy, not to mention the security of the nuclear stockpile, so the World Bank remained engaged in Russia. Even in its moment of weakness, Russia dealt with the Bretton Woods institutions from a position of strength. Neither Boris Yeltsin nor Vladimir Putin applied the 'shock therapies' that were so readily embraced in Eastern Europe (e.g., Poland), and the United States concurred. Until now, China has resisted Bank 'recommendation' to allow the yuan to free float; instead, Beijing has been steadfast in keeping its currency non-convertible, in spite of the impact this is having on world trade because of the falling dollar (to which the yuan is fixed).

In sum, Bank policy typically reflects not only neo-liberal ideology, but also realpolitik, that is, power asymmetry between the Bank and borrowing countries, which varies in magnitude. Large developing countries, such as China, or developed ones, such as Russia, have greater clout in negotiating with the Bank than small, underdeveloped countries, but even the latter may stand up to the Bank (to a point), if their elites feel that Bank-imposed policies are likely to cause them to lose power. And since the World Bank is ultimately in the business of lending to earn money (not poverty reduction, as the rhetoric goes), it cannot be entirely oblivious to borrowers, especially if they can make payments on their debt.

Conclusion

Part II of the study has tried to develop a theoretical framework of the World Bank that brings together organization theory, especially systems theory and bureaucratic politics, rational choice theory and ideology. It has tried to show that ideology does not exist in a social vacuum; where the Bank is concerned, it operates within an organizational environment and a larger environment that, at any time, serve to constrain its application. Organizations like the external environment when they can use it as a source of support—political, financial, whatever. This leads them to engage in boundary spanning, that is to say, reaching out, in rhizome-like fashion, to borrow from Jean-François Bayart, to find the 'nutrients' needed for survival.[112]

Boundary spanning often leads organizations to take on tasks for which they are not particularly well suited (the expansion of the Bank from reconstruction to development). At the same time, organizations loathe the external environment when it threatens their internal operations, thus their tendency to engage in buffering, which is their defence against 'intrusion'. The limits imposed by bureaucratic politics on one hand and extra-bureaucratic politics on the other explain gaps between Bank rhetoric and policy, and, at times, may even contribute to policy shifts that, on the surface, contravene Bank ideology. It devolves to Bank presidents, as it does any chief executive officer (CEO) of a large corporation, to play the crucial role of balancing interests within the Bank on one hand and pressure from the external environment on the other. Thus the zigzagging of Bank lending policy over the decades since its founding can be seen as an attempt to jettison neo-liberal ideology, bureaucratic politics, a preference for gargantuanism inside the Bank (which is also a result of the way the Bank raises private funds) with the realities of the external environment, which is complex and volatile.

This means that neo-liberalism can sometimes be temporarily sidelined in favour of populist policies, until a 'policy window' makes its return possible. While Bank ideology has been consistently neo-liberal, the Bank has had to evince flexibility in (neo-liberal) policy, because of the external environment and, once again, bureaucratic politics. The World Bank has to be all things to all people: it must keep its largest contributors satisfied, if not happy; it must maintain private investor confidence in its (AAA) bonds; it must pay some attention to its customers (though not as much to those that cannot raise funds on private capital markets, attract direct foreign investment or are otherwise in deep economic crisis); it must be sensitive to how it is perceived by other multilateral organizations and social activists; and its policies must be anchored in an intellectual framework that is consonant with its real mission but at the same time do not seem overly dogmatic. To do all of the above, the World Bank must remain above fray, or constantly reinvent itself, at least in rhetoric. Its renewal is a necessary condition for its survival.

In the 1950s modernization theory and free-market ideology coincided; as a result, Bank lending policy was characterized by orthodoxy. The intellectual ferment of the 1960s and 1970s, not to mention international politics (i.e., decolonization, the Vietnam War, the environmental movement, etc.), was less favourable to neo-liberalism. In response, the Bank co-opted some of the demands of the time and even reorganized itself internally. Specifically, its atomization in 1960, into IBRD and IDA, was a classic organizational attempt at adaptation to an external environment that was changing from colonies to independent states and in which the line in the sand between West and East had moved from Berlin to Saigon (hence 'defensive modernization'). Through

IBRD the Bank remained true to its original mission: raising funds on capital markets and lending them to 'credit worthy' countries to finance capital intensive projects with high returns on investment, which it had always preferred; through IDA the Bank looked like a development institution, lending money for 'softer' projects, thereby placating critics and allowing Third World state elites to deliver on the promises of decolonization. This latter side of 'defensive modernization' resulted in significant investments in the poor, especially in agriculture, through the 1970s. Its real aim, however, was not more equitable distribution of wealth within and between countries, but rather to pre-empt the implementation of rising demands in this direction and maintain neo-liberal hegemony.

Not surprisingly, Bank investment in the Third World poor failed, nowhere more so than in agriculture, where technology transfer did not increase rural productivity, then widely touted as the way out of poverty. The return to overt economic orthodoxy in the 1980s was undergirded by this bitter experience in the Third World, rightist political victories in the First World (USA, UK), and the disintegration of Soviet-style political economies later in the decade in the Second World, which made it safe, once again, for the Bank to rediscover its (neo-liberal) roots and reject adumbrated forms of market economies. Structural adjustment programs (SAPs) were the means by which the World Bank sought first to recast the Third World (and then the Second World) so as to realize the goal for which it was created, and to which it was committed all along: a free-market-based global economic order.

The disappointing results of neo-liberal policies in the 1990s, the AIDS pandemic, the collapse of peripheral capitalist states, the emergence of articulate publics, especially in Africa, and, perhaps, the events of 91101 may have forced a retreat to a less doctrinaire posture in which states play a more prominent, but still subservient, role, in Bank worldview. This latest shift can clearly be discerned, once more, in Bank rhetoric, which professes deep interest in the amelioration of negative social conditions (i.e., poverty reduction) in borrowing countries. However, as the next (co-written) section shows, the rhetoric is, once more, betrayed by the reality of lending policy. It will demonstrate that (a) most Bank funds do not go to the world's poorest countries and (b) those that do do not support projects that most directly affect the poor inside these countries.

Part III

World Bank Lending in Empirical Perspective

(co-authored with Olga Prokopovych)

All of the data used in this study were extracted from documents, including web sites, of these international institutions: the World Bank, United Nations, Freedom House and Transparency International. The advantage of using these sources should be obvious: access. We have not had to reinvent the wheel; the reader can easily check for herself the authenticity of our data. We chose to scrutinize data produced by the very institution under study, a necessary step, in our view, to the deconstruction effort in which we are engaged in this investigation. We examined data from 1984 to 2002. This has at least one major advantage: the period is sufficiently lengthy (18 years) to detect variations and justify generalizations. Bank behaviour here cannot be said to be spasmodic and 'unrepresentative' of what the Bank says it is about (poverty reduction).

Our first task was to answer the following part of the research question: Does World Bank lending go to the world's poorest countries? Methodologically, this is a straightforward exercise. We examined Bank lending worldwide to see who its recipients were from 1984 to 2002. We used a modified version of the 2002 United Nations Human Development Index (UN-HDI) to classify some recipient countries. Here is how we did so and why. Officially, poor countries are those listed in the UN-HDI as having a Low Human Development index. They are at and below 138 on a list of 173 countries. Unofficially, however, we think that the number of poor countries is much larger than 35. Thus, we decided to divide countries in the Medium Human Development category, which precedes the Low Human Development category, into High Medium Human Development and Low Medium Human Development countries. We did this because countries in the Medium Human Development category show wide income and other variations, from Mexico

(54), with a GDP per capita of 9,023 USD, to Congo (136), with a GDP per capita of 825 USD. We split this category into the sub-categories of High Medium Human Development and Low Medium Human Development, while keeping the Low Development and High Human Development categories of the UN intact. For a country that is in the Low Medium Human Development sub-category may, in fact, be closer to one in the Low Human Development category than one in the High Medium Human Development sub-category. For example, the per capita income difference between Zambia — Low Human Development — and Congo — Low-Medium Human Development — is only 45 USD, whereas that between Congo and Mexico — High Medium Human Development — is a whopping 8,198 USD. The split between the two sub-categories (i.e., High Medium and Low Medium) occurs very near the median of 54 and 137, which is the 96th country on the list. Below are total Bank lending disbursements per annum by categories of countries (according to our modified version of United Nations Human Development Index) in nominal and percentage terms, as well as averages over the 18-year period.

Table 2 shows that, from 1984 to 2002, the poorest countries in the world, i.e., those in the Low Human Development category (from Pakistan at 138 to Sierra Leone at 173), as defined by the UN, received, on average, 16 percent of Bank (IBRD and IDA) lending. More than 60 percent of Bank lending during this period, in fact, goes to countries in the Medium Human Development Index category, with those in the High Medium Human Development sub-category (our classification) receiving as much in percentage terms as those in the Low Medium Human Development sub-category (each received 36 percent of Bank lending). Even if one were to collapse countries in the Low Medium Human Development sub-category (our classification) with those in the Low Human Development category (UN), the combined average would only represent 52 percent of Bank lending to countries containing at least 80 percent of the world's people. Furthermore, Bank lending also went to High Human Development countries from 1984 to 2002. In fact, there is a only a 4 percent difference in average Bank lending to High Human Development countries (12 percent) and Low Human Development countries (16 percent). Does World Bank lending support projects that most directly affect the poor in poor countries, namely: health, education, agriculture, water, sanitation and flood protection?[113] Answering this part of the question is not as straightforward as the first. Extensive explanations are in order.

Time and resources limited our sample size to 25 countries.[114] Therefore, it was crucial that we had a sample 'representative' of poor countries. This meant, once again, reconfiguring the UN's Human Development Index in such a way

Table 2: World Bank Lending (1984–2002)

Year	High HDI	(%)	High M HDI	(%)	Low MHDI	(%)	Low HDI	(%)	Total
1984	963	8	3,136	27	5,893	49	2,115	17	12,108
1985	1,806	12	4,743	30	7,012	45	2,154	14	15,715
1986	1,691	10	5,884	36	5,407	33	3,299	20	16,280
1987	1,579	9	4,898	29	8,406	49	2,290	13	17,173
1988	2,280	12	4,959	27	7,257	39	4,146	22	18,642
1989	1,654	8	7,019	33	9,162	43	3,724	17	21,559
1990	2,199	11	7,196	35	6,934	34	4,128	20	20,457
1991	3,545	16	5,636	25	9,477	43	3,507	16	22,166
1992	1,950	9	8,136	38	8,004	37	3,411	16	21,501
1993	3,685	18	5,507	27	8,807	43	2,411	12	20,409
1994	2,009	9	9,023	39	8,198	36	3,769	16	22,998
1995	3,013	14	7,089	33	8,386	40	2,708	13	21,195
1996	1,775	9	7,973	39	8,884	43	2,055	10	20,687
1997	5,223	22	9,039	38	6,520	28	2,726	12	23,508
1998	8,944	29	10,665	34	8,398	27	3,301	11	*31,308
1999	962	5	8,549	44	7,005	36	2,896	15	19,412
2000	1,039	4	15,304	61	5,617	22	3,245	13	25,205
2001	1,349	8	7,175	40	5,308	30	4,147	23	17,979
2002	545	3	7,217	42	4,882	28	4,727	27	17,370
Total	46,211	12	139,146	36	139,554	36	60,759	16	385,670
Average	2,432	12	7,323	36	7,345	36	3,198	16	20,298

Note: all nominal figures are in billions.

* Bank lending in 1998 seems abnormally high. We attribute this to the Asian Financial Crisis but we are not sure why.

Source: www.worldbank.org

that countries that are alike the Low Human Development countries (138 and up) are represented. They happen to be the countries that are on the low end of the Medium Human Development category. Thus, from now on Low Human Development countries in this study mean those that are at 96th and up on the UN's HDI 2002 report, rather than at 138th and up. We readily acknowledge, here and now, that ours is not a randomized sample, with all of the scientific limitations that this entails.

As always in statistical research, we were interested not in the items (i.e., individual countries) of the sample but the population (in the statistical sense). In choosing the countries we were sensitive to including those that have the same characteristics as the 'average' characteristics in the population (again, in the statistical sense) of poor countries. The universe of poor countries is of course very wide; as a result, we made sure that we accounted for as many of the variations that exist among them as possible in our sample. We were sensitive to geography, size (as determined by population), resource endowments (i.e., whether countries are natural resource-rich or natural resource-poor), economic profile (whether countries have economies that are overwhelmingly agrarian, industrial or service-based), 'stateness' (whether countries have functioning states or failed ones), political regimes (whether countries are democratic or authoritarian) and corruption perception (as classified by Transparency International).[115]

We examined IBRD and IDA lending in 10 areas (14 if one decouples the 4 clusters): law and administration, industry and trade, education, health, finance, agriculture, water sanitation and flood protection, transportation, energy and mining, and telecommunications. Why these? Because together they comprise over 90 percent of World Bank lending to developing countries. Hence, what we are talking about here is not lending to marginal projects, but rather the core projects upon which the Bank has staked its legitimacy. Health, education, agriculture, water sanitation and flood protection are assumed to directly affect the poor and deemed crucial indicators of 'human development', not by us but the World Bank and major donors. Their inclusion in a major study of World Bank lending allows for an assessment of whether rhetoric on the Potomac matches financial commitment in the Sahel or Andes, among other regions. We were fortunate enough to find data on Bank lending divided between IDA and IBRD. This is not a trivial occurrence, for IDA is specifically mandated to assist the world's poor.

Tables 3 and 4 show average IDA and IBRD financing to the 10 project areas mentioned above during the period under study (1984–2002) for all 25 countries.

Table 3: IDA-Financed Projects (1984-2002)

	1	2	3	4	5	6	7	8	9	10
China	7	8	14	14	3	37	12	3	2	1
Bolivia	26	5	10	15	2	6	8	26	1	0
Egypt	6	13	17	23	15	25	1	0	0	0
Honduras	21	5	14	17	2	12	3	20	5	1
Nicaragua	36	2	8	14	9	6	5	20	0	1
India	11	2	20	25	0	21	10	7	4	0
Cambodia	31	5	5	25	0	5	8	13	8	0
Pakistan	9	4	23	9	12	23	14	3	4	0
Laos	17	7	8	10	4	5	2	31	11	5
Yemen	10	1	17	14	1	9	28	14	6	0
Bangladesh	8	10	10	14	9	4	7	23	14	0
Haiti	10	8	3	35	1	8	12	23	0	0
Tanzania	21	1	10	5	9	3	4	23	19	4
Zambia	21	21	7	9	5	11	7	9	10	0
Côte d'Ivoire	26	13	10	11	1	8	1	20	9	1
Central African Republic	40	2	9	11	11	0	6	10	0	
Chad	20	1	3	18	0	9	4	36	10	0
Guinea Bissau	24	5	8	18	3	2	2	20	20	0
Ethiopia	13	8	8	31	0	8	3	21	18	0
Burkina Faso	22	0	14	21	0	14	18	12	1	0
Mozambique	33	8	8	7	10	3	5	22	4	0
Sierra Leone	17	7	1	15	5	4	17	25	9	0
Average	**19**	**6**	**10**	**16**	**5**	**10**	**7**	**17**	**7**	**1**

Where: 1 - Law and Public Administration; 2 - Industry and Trade; 3 - Education; 4 - Health; 5 - Finance; 6 - Agriculture; 7 - Water, sanitation and flood protection; Dependent variables 8 - Transportation; 9 - Energy and mining; 10 - Telecommunications.

Note: All numbers are expressed in percentages of total IDA financing for each country. Morocco and Guatemala were excluded because they had no reported IDA financing during this period, as was Jordan, which had one reported project in law and justice in 1999. **Source**: www.worldbank.org Retrieved on May 5, 2003.

Table 4: IBRD-Financed Projects (1984-2002)

	1	2	3	4	5	6	7	8	9	10
China	3	5	0	1	1	9	14	36	28	2
Jordan	12	12	20	7	11	7	9	9	8	2
Bolivia	0	0	0	0	0	0	0	0	100	0
Egypt	6	11	6	0	3	35	3	3	31	3
India	4	5	0	1	1	5	7	28	46	3
Pakistan	3	7	0	0	17	6	0	12	55	3
Chad	0	0	0	0	0	0	0	12	84	4
Guatemala	32	5	19	8	29	0	2	13	0	0
Morocco	9	9	9	11	10	20	9	21	2	0
AVERAGE	**7**	**5**	**4**	**3**	**8**	**9**	**4**	**16**	**43**	**2**

Where: 1 – Law and Public Administration; 2 – Industry and Trade; 3 – Education;

4 – Health; 5 – Finance; 6 – Agriculture; 7 – Water, sanitation and flood protection;

8 – Transportation; 9 – Energy and mining; 10 – Telecommunications.

Note: All numbers are expressed in percentages of total IDA financing for each country. Even though Bolivia had only one reported IBRD-financed project in 1997, we decided to include Bolivia, because of the importance of mining to the Bolivian economy.

Source: www.worldbank.org. Retrieved on May 5, 2003.

Tables 3 and 4 show that two sectors—energy and mining and transportation—account for much of IDA and IBRD-financed projects in the countries in the study. Specifically, energy and mining represent a combined average of 50 percent of the projects financed by IBRD and IDA. Transportation took, on average, a further 32 percent of combined IBRD and IDA-financed projects. (Yes, gargantuanism is alive and well.) Telecommunications received the least financing from either agency, probably because the Bank has preferred the privatization of state-owned telecommunications companies to their restructuring. But the most revealing finding is that, in spite of their oft-stated commitment to poverty reduction in the Third World, IBRD and IDA financing of projects that most directly benefit the poor is relatively modest.[116]

Tables 3 and 4 show combined IDA and IBRD financing of education, health, agriculture, water sanitation and flood protection to be, respectively: 14, 19, 19 and 11 percent. Again, this was the period (1984-2002) when the World Bank made poverty reduction its mantra; but rhetorical commitment in Bank literature does not seem to match financial support on the ground, even by the Bank's own data.[117] IBRD, in particular, continues to have a preference for large-scale, capital-intensive infrastructure projects (i.e., energy and mining and transportation), possibly at the expense of those connected to poverty reduction or human development (i.e., education, health and agriculture).

Tables 3 and 4 also show some differences in lending patterns not only across sector projects but also among borrowing countries. Specifically, the lower the standing of countries on the Human Development Index (HDI), the lower the level of lending to poverty-related projects (this observation will be brought in sharper relief in the correlation and regression tables and discussions below). Thus, Chad (ranked 166) received no IBRD funding for education, health, agriculture, water sanitation and flood protection; it received IDA funding for projects in these sectors at the following percentages: 3 (education), 18 (health), 9 (agriculture), and 4 (water sanitation and flood protection). This is significant because IDA was initially created to deal with abjectly poor countries such as Chad.

By contrast, energy and mining and transportation (i.e., road construction and maintenance) accounted for 96 percent of IBRD lending to Chad during the period, while these sectors accounted for 46 percent of IDA financing.118 In China (ranked 96), education, health, agriculture, water sanitation and flood protection accounted for 14, 14, 37 and 12 percent of IDA-financed projects from 1984-2002, in other words, more than 3 times above the average for agriculture for the countries in the study, 4 percentage points higher than the average for education, 2 percentage points less than the average for health, and 5 percentage points higher than the average for water sanitation and flood protection, yet China has the best HDI ranking among countries in the study. As for IBRD, its financing of projects in the aforementioned sectors in China is stingy, compared to that of IDA, but IBRD is generally more generous toward China than it is Chad (in fact, considerably more so where agriculture and water sanitation and flood protection are concerned).

Lest we stand accused of singling out cases that support our contention, namely, that the World Bank continues to show preference for capital-intensive infrastructure projects (gargantuanism) over poverty reduction and to the extent that it is interested in the latter, it is only for certain (not-so-poor) countries, we shall take two more pairs of countries. In Bolivia (ranked 114), education, health, agriculture and water sanitation and flood protection accounted for, respectively, 10, 15, 6 and 8 percent of IDA financing, while there is no reported IBRD support to projects in these areas. In Pakistan (ranked 138), education, health, agriculture and water sanitation and flood protection accounted for, respectively, 23, 9, 23 and 14 percent of IDA financing, while IBRD lending was limited to one project area (agriculture at 6 percent of total average lending). Thus, in Pakistan the World Bank—specifically IDA— provided greater and more even support for poverty reduction projects than it did in Bolivia; in fact, only in one area, health, is average Bank funding in Bolivia greater than in Pakistan.

The last pair consists of Egypt (115) and India (124), although these two countries are much closer to each other on the HDI ranking than the first two pairs. In Egypt, IDA funding for education, health, agriculture, water sanitation and flood protection is 17, 23, 25, and 1 percent of total financing on average from 1984 to 2002. IBRD funding for projects in these areas was 6, 0, 35 and 3 percent during the same period. In India (124), IDA funding for education, health, agriculture, water sanitation and flood protection was 20, 25, 21 and 10 percent of total financing on average from 1984 to 2002. IBRD funding for projects in these areas in India was, on average, 0,1,5 and 7 percent of total financing from 1984 to 2004. In sum, the World Bank, especially IDA, was more generous toward India in the financing of poverty reduction projects than it was toward Egypt, but, once again, the two countries are so close on the HDI ranking that it cannot be said their position made a difference to their funding levels. In fact, we think that there are other, more compelling, factors in the disbursement of World Bank funds than HDI ranking (more on these in the next tables).

To assess the importance of variables, including HDI ranking, to Bank funding, we performed correlation and regression analyses. Once again, the variables we accounted for were: resources, 'stateness', HID ranking, size, corruption and regime type. Tables 5 and 6 contain the results of our findings; they shall be examined in turn.

As Table 5 shows, some variables are more strongly correlated to World Bank (IDA and IBRD) funding than others; we shall examine the variables that are positively correlated first and those that are negatively correlated second.

Resources and IDA/IBRD Funding

Table 5 shows a strong positive correlation between resources and IDA and IBRD funding at 0.50 and 0.53 respectively. In other words, the richer the country in natural resources, the higher the likelihood of its receiving Bank support; this is especially the case for IBRD. There could be two reasons for this. As asserted earlier, the World Bank may be inclined to lend money to countries that can repay their debt; thus, the more they are endowed in resources, the higher their credit worthiness and the more attractive they are to the Bank as borrowers. In addition, the World Bank, especially IBRD, may be more interested, for lack of a more elegant English term, in 'valorizing' the physical assets of countries than in directly helping them to achieve human development or reduce poverty. We infer this from IBRD's tendency to fund capital-intensive, infrastructure projects. No matter the reason, countries that are well endowed in natural resources will, ceteris paribus, attract Bank funding more easily than those that are not.

'Stateness' and IDA/IBRD Funding

Table 5 shows a strong correlation between IDA and IBRD funding and stateness at coefficient levels of 0.72 and 0.77 respectively. These were the strongest correlation coefficients between two different variables. They suggest that the World Bank tends to lend money to countries with working states, that is, states with political leaders and civil servants who can, among other things, prepare proposals and serve as interlocuteurs de poids (valuable interlocutors) before the Bank. In Bankspeak, institutional capacity; how much in financial terms will be assessed in the regression table.

TICP Index and HDI Ranking

Table 5 shows a positive correlation (0.62) between the TICP index and HID ranking. In other words, the higher the Corruption Perception Index (i.e., the more corrupt the country), the higher the score on the HDI ranking (i.e., the

Table 5: Correlation

	Resources	IDA funding	IBRD funding	Stateness civil servants	HDI Ranking	Size (pop)	TICP Index (Corruption)	FH Ranking Regime
Resources	1.0000							
IDA funding	0.4599	1.0000						
IBRD funding	0.5193	0.9643	1.0000					
Stateness	0.4782	0.7175	0.7820	1.0000				
HDI rank	-0.2160	-0.4033	-0.4718	-0.3923	1.0000			
Size(pop.)	0.1995	0.5594	0.4785	0.6052	0.0035	1.0000		
TICP Index	-0.2451	-0.2974	-0.3552	-0.2761	0.5799	-0.2465	1.0000	
FH Ranking	-0.2170	-0.0852	-0.1082	-0.2662	0.4141	0.1159	0.1948	1.0000

poorer the country). Although one should refrain from drawing firm causal inferences from correlations, one may, nevertheless, in this case conjecture that extreme corruption may have corrosive effects on poverty reduction as the latter relates to education, health, agriculture (in other words, food production) and water. This is not an unreasonable hypothesis; funds that are 'intercepted' by elites for private use do not reach their intended targets, who are then left to wallow in ignorance, disease, hunger and thirst.

Size and IDA/IBRD Funding

Table 5 shows a positive correlation between size and IDA and IBRD funding — higher for IDA — and size. Large countries, as determined by the size of their population, tend to receive more funding from the World Bank than medium-sized and small countries, although we suspect that factors other than size may be at play (such as, for example, the fact that large countries like China and India have working states and rank among the least corrupt in the sample).

HDI Ranking and IDA/IBRD Funding

On the other hand, Table 5 shows a negative correlation between HDI ranking and IDA and IBRD funding at -0.40 and -0.46 respectively.[119] In other words, the higher a country's HDI ranking (i.e., the poorer it is), the lower is IDA and, especially, IBRD funding. (We discussed the significance of this finding earlier in this article and will return to it later.)

Freedom House Ranking (i.e., political regimes) and IDA/IBRD Funding

In the 1990s a democratic 'third wave' engulfed the world, beginning with the fall of the Berlin Wall and the eventual collapse of the former Soviet Union. In some of the world's most vulnerable, or dependent, countries, the rush to democratize was based on expectations of a so-called democracy bonus, that is, countries whose democratization efforts met with approval from the 'donor' community thought that they would receive new aid or have past debt cancelled. The World Bank probably contributed to the environment when it added good governance to its wish list of what poor countries needed to do to jumpstart their economies, and former French president François Mitterrand explicitly linked French aid to democratic reform. Table 5 shows no correlation between regime type and IDA/IBRD funding. In fact, the World Bank does not appear to allocate resources for democracy enhancement, although it is possible that

Bank funding for this purpose may be embedded in other projects (e.g., Law and Administration). Simply put, poor democratizing countries received neither bonus nor dividend, at least not directly and not from the World Bank.

Regression

Because correlation does not necessarily beget causation, and because we wanted to measure more precisely the relationship between variables, we decided to run some bi-variate regression analyses. Table 6 shows the findings.

Table 6: Results of Bi-Variate Regressions

Independent variables \ Dependent variables	IDA financing Coefficients (t-score in parenthesis)	IBRD financing Coefficients (t-score in parenthesis)
Resources	2,550,000,000	2,950,000,000
	(2.75)*	(3.01)**
Number of Central Government Civil Servants	4,855 (4.49)**	5,815 (5.47)**
Number of Government Employees in Education	3,498 (8.84)**	4,619 (19.34)**
Number of Government Employees in Health	6,527 (11.14)**	7,012 (10.05)**
HDI Ranking	-71,400,000	-89,200,000
	(-2.10)*	(-2.51)*
Transparency International Corruption Perception Index	-73,300,000 (-1.69)	-89,400,000 (-1.94)
Freedom House Ranking	-539,000,000	-743,000,000
	(-0.44)	(-0.56)
Number of Observations	25	25

* Significant at .05 level

** Significant at .01 level

Resources and IDA/IBRD Funding

Table 6 suggests that the more resources a country has, the more likely it will receive World Bank funding. Specifically, as countries move from being 'resource poor' to 'resource rich', they can expect IDA financing to increase by more than 2.5 billion USD and IBRD financing to nearly 3 billion USD, with respective t-scores of 2.75 and 3.01 (row 1).

'Stateness' and IDA/IBRD Funding

As stated earlier, how much state a country has matters for Bank funding. Specifically, Table 6 suggests that each additional civil servant in the central government results in 4,760 USD in IDA aid and 5,545 USD in IBRD aid (row 2). Thus, the larger the number of civil servants in borrowing countries, the bigger the aid from IDA and IBRD. Further, given the relative weight of the coefficients, each additional civil servant has a greater impact on IBRD funding than IDA funding. This is consistent with the rest of the data and our knowledge of the two entities, which show IBRD to be more 'business like' than IDA.

In Table 6 we decided to examine state capacity in two specific sectors for which data were available: education and health (respectively, rows 3 and 4). The table suggests that with each additional civil servant in the education sector, IDA funding would increase by 1,905 USD and IBRD funding by 2,041 USD. Again, there is a difference in the relative weight of the coefficients with increased capacity having a greater impact on IBRD funding than IDA funding. Where health is concerned, each additional health worker results in 6,620 USD in IDA funding and 7,071 USD in IBRD funding. These results all but confirm one of the key assertions made earlier: 'stateness' matter in the financial relationship between countries and the World Bank. (The reader should be made aware that numerical data on 'stateness' cover the period between 1991-2000, rather than the entire time period of the study, 1984-2002. If we had complete data, we probably would have had slightly different results, but the high t-scores and coefficients give us confidence that this would not have changed the main finding.)

HDI Ranking and IDA/IBRD Funding

The finding we are about to discuss is, for the purposes of the study, perhaps the most important or revealing. As stated earlier, HDI ranking tends to be inversely related to IDA and IBRD funding (this is consistent with Table 5). The regression results show that funding from IDA and IBRD decreases (or increases), respectively, by 71,400,000 USD and 89, 200,000 USD each time a country's human development index (HDI) worsens (or improves) (row 5). Thus, the poorest countries — those with the highest scores on the HDI ranking — received less funding from either agency than the not-so-poor countries. The implication of this finding cannot be overstated. Simply put, in spite of official claims, the World Bank cannot be counted upon to reduce poverty or bring about human development in the world's poorest countries — or at least in the poorest countries included in the study — for these are not the countries to which Bank funding typically goes. The policy reversal that would be necessary to address this anomaly would imply (a) channelling the flow of aid to the countries that need it most — i.e., those with a high score on the HDI ranking — and (b) recalibrating the flow of aid to human development or poverty-related projects, even if countries suffer from a lack of civil service capacity in these areas.

TICP Index and IDA/IBRD Funding

Table 6 shows that the perception of corruption in a country, as listed in the Transparency International Corruption Perception (TICP) Index, has a negative impact on IDA and IBRD funding.[120] Each increase in a country's corruption perception ranking can be expected to result in a loss of 73,300,000 USD in IDA funding and 89,400,000 USD in IBRD funding (row 6). In sum, where countries are concerned, corruption — nay, crime — does not pay.

Freedom House Ranking (i.e., political regimes) and IDA/IBRD Funding

Finally, as with Table 5, Table 6 shows that regime type has no impact on Bank funding.

Conclusion

Reforming or Rethinking the World Bank?

I will be parsimonious in summarizing the conclusion of the joint foray into World Bank lending in Part III: World Bank rhetoric regarding poverty reduction does not match the reality of World Bank lending. The world's poorest countries received only 16 percent of Bank lending on average between 1984 and 2002. Instead, I will focus on the following questions: What is to be done, so that poor countries and projects that benefit the Third World poor are funded? What is to be done about the World Bank? Here I admit that the conclsuion is intended to provoke thoughts, rather than propose fully developed solutions. I believe, however, that empirical evidence already exists for radical changes in Bank lending policy to be considered, and perhaps for alternatives to the Bank itself to be developed.

There has to be a major shift in the way projects that directly benefit the poor are conceived. Neo-liberalism assumes that every good, save perhaps national defence, policing and justice, is a private good, which means that they must be produced and delivered by private actors on a for-profit basis. Thus, health care, education and extension services have been 'privatized', as part of the requirements of adjustment lending. In fact, these are mostly public goods that require state participation, if their delivery is to approach optimality and if standards and safety are not to be called into question. In Cameroon, primary and secondary school enrolment went down after cost recovery was introduced in the 1990s, so did child immunity.[121] Poor parents could not afford the fees to send their children to school or health clinics. The social character of public goods, such as education, health care, extension services and environmental protection must be rediscovered, so that adequate funding for their delivery may be forthcoming.

As long as the World Bank thinks that nearly everything can be somehow privatized, the gap in funding between social goods that directly benefit the poor and large infrastructure projects can be expected to endure, perhaps even widen. This is not to say that there is no role for private actors in education, health care and the like. There is. In 1991 I witnessed first-hand the willingness of livestock farmers to purchase drugs for their herds in northern Cameroon. As a result, veterinary drug supply improved, when drugs had nearly disappeared from the shelves of the government parastatal (Office Pharma-ceutique Vétérinaire, OPV) in charge of their distribution.[122] Private universities have mushroomed throughout Africa in recent years, and may be playing an important role in opening higher education to groups previously excluded from university (e.g., women and older workers).

But it has to be recognized that the benefits of education do not accrue only to individual 'consumers'; there is also a high value to society of an educated citizenry. The same applies, perhaps even more so, to health care and reforestation. A market approach insures neither that these things will be provided at all, nor that significant numbers of individuals will not be excluded from their benefits. Markets are great at producing some goods but notoriously lousy in insuring equitable distribution. Once the limits of markets are recognized in the public goods sector, it is not difficult, even for the World Bank, to accept that the state must play a key role in this sector in levelling the playing field and in monitoring standards. This prise de conscience should then open the way for the (re)financing of projects in the aforementioned areas and in countries that need them the most.

In sum, there has to be an ideological paradigm shift at the Bank (not just rhetoric to that effect), one that is genuinely committed to reducing the poverty that market reforms tend to create. A pro-poor World Bank is possible only if poor countries have a greater voice inside the Bank. The current governance structure of the World Bank is clearly more suited for the realities of the immediate post-World War II era than those of the new millennium. To its credit, the World Bank has continually adjusted its rhetoric, and sometime even its policies, but has yet to seriously consider internal restructuring so as to become more democratic.[123] This would involve either enlarging the size of the board of executive directors, so Newly Industrialized Countries (NICs) and developing countries are individually represented, or changing the terms upon which current executive directors serve at the World Bank. Since practically all World Bank lending activities take place in the Third World, the president of the World Bank ought to be someone familiar with the Third World. The practice of appointing an American to head the Bank should be ended forthwith. Instead, the presidency of the World Bank, like the UN general secretariat, should be rotated among the major geographic regions of the world, so each continent gets to have one of its nationals serves as Bank presidents (and IMF managing directors).

The World Bank has been able to hide behind the veil of lofty rhetoric to conceal the ugly realities of its lending policy, which have wreaked havoc on the Third World poor. It has been able to do this in part because of the secrecy under which the Bank operates. Few people have access to the minutes of the board of executive directors' meetings, where decisions are made. Such decisions are reported collectively; thus, it is not possible to know how specific directors vote on policy issues. Bank lending policy may be made in Washington D.C. but the ripple effects are felt throughout the Third World. Yet most citizens there have no idea how (and what) 'their' governments negotiate with the World Bank; indeed, in some countries the in-country resident of the World Bank (and IMF) has virtual veto power over decisions taken by national leaders and institutions.[124] In Ghana, a decision by the government, approved by Parliament, to provide modest protection to local industry was quietly shelved in 2003, after the local representative of the IMF apparently objected. Interestingly, this decision complied with the rules of the World Trade Organization (WTO), but not those of the IMF.

Third World people need to know what deals are being struck on their behalf behind closed doors — deals for which they will have to pay for generations to come. Greater transparency in negotiations between the Bank and Third World governments may make the Bank live up to its commitment to poverty reduction. In addition, executive directors should routinely inform their constituencies on how they vote on policy proposals;[125] they may even be called to publicly testify before the legislature of individual countries they represent. They should also pay regular visits to these countries and consult with their finance and monetary authorities on matters of common interest.

The World Bank's embrace of PRSPs is, in theory, laudable. The emphasis on participation in and ownership of programs by stakeholders in borrowing countries should elicit no objection. But one has to wonder: Does the democratization of projects for which donor support is to be sought have a more sinister purpose (i.e., to legitimize the lending conditionalities that are increasingly attached to PRSPs)? And what happens when civil society groups that are called to participate in PRSPs do not sing the tune of the World Bank? Democracy at any level always connotes uncertainty. Is the World Bank prepared to support poverty alleviation projects that genuinely relieve poverty, or reject market-based reforms?

Let there be no doubt: reform of the World Bank is unlikely to occur in the absence of political struggles by the grassroots. The Bank's commitment to neo-liberalism is long-standing, and given the current hegemony of that ideology, it would be naïve in the extreme to think that a change of heart will occur at the summit of world financial power. But change is possible — always. At the start of the 1980s Apartheid South Africa was one of the safest places for multina-tional corporations and pension funds to invest. By the middle of the decade social activists had forced many an investor to 'divest' from South Africa, in 1989 Nelson Mandela was freed and in 1994 South Africa was under majority rule for the first time in 300 years.

The increasing vocality of international civil society, as reflected in massive demonstrations at the annual meetings of the World Bank and its sister organizations (IMF and WTO), could yet force a major shift in lending policies. Such a shift should entail the cancellation, outright and without preconditions, of past debt, the interest on which, not the repayment of principals, is preventing debtor countries from investing in the poor. There is a direct connection among Bank lending, Third World debt and reduced social expenditures: ceteris paribus, the more countries owe (as a percentage of their Gross Domestic Product, GDP) the more they pay in debt servicing (also as a percentage of their Gross Domestic Product, GDP) and the fewer the resources available for social investment aimed at poverty reduction.

Too, there are alternatives to Bank lending, and more, still, can be imagined. The world's poor need not remain confined to the chicaneries of the World Bank. Regional development banks still exist. They can lend more to the poorest countries and support projects that benefit the poor inside these countries. Before these alternatives are seriously considered, however, further research is needed, to ascertain whether their lending preferences are any different from those of the World Bank. Future research should aim at a comparative analysis of lending policies by the major development institutions, with due allowance for their stated mission, geographic coverage, the size of their budget and nature (whether they are multilateral or governmental — e.g., respectively, the World Bank and USAID).

In addition, not-for-profit, and even for-profit, lending organizations, committed to helping the poor, can be created. They could come into being if rich countries like the United States would agree to devote a portion of their GDP or national budget (say, 1 to 3 percent) to development aid. Along the same line, the French proposal for a world tax for development ought to be explored. These organizations could operate either on a regional or in-country basis. Grameen banks were started in Bangladesh, and their success in lending

74

to the poor has been so overwhelming that equivalent institutions are springing up elsewhere (Latin America).[126] The World Bank's preference, as I stated at the beginning, has been for gargantuanism: mega-projects with high visibility, prestige and solid return to investment. Yet it is widely acknowledged that the Third World poor is especially active in micro-enterprises, even though paved roads may facilitate the taking of goods to market.

Micro-enterprise lending at very low interest rates may be one of the most effective ways of reducing poverty in the Third World, for, unlike some governments, not only does the Third World poor pay back her debt, thereby insuring the availability of funds for future borrowers, she is only showing an adumbration (e.g., hawking) of the entrepreneurial spirit. Under the circumstances, not even 'primitive' accumulation of capital is possible; with micro-lending, along with training in management and accounting, the sky may be the only limit.

From the beginning the commitment of the World Bank to lending only to elites, may have severely limited its ability to reach the masses. Having served elites for all of its history, the World Bank may now be ill-equipped to serve ordinary citizens, especially the poorest. The creation of alternative lending organizations may thus be a sine qua non for reaching the Third World poor and alleviating her lot.

Notes

1. 'The World Bank's mission is to reduce poverty and improve living standards through sustainable growth and investment in people.' Http: //www.worldbank.org/-poverty/mission/index.htm, extracted July 5, 2003. What is the World Bank?, the de facto mission statement of the Bank on the Internet, states: 'Along with the rest of the development community, the World Bank centres its efforts on the Millennium Development Goals, agreed to by UN members in 2000 and aimed at sustainable poverty reduction.' What is the World Bank? http://web.worldbank.org, extracted July 5, 2003.

2. Vivian Forrester, *L'horreur économique*, Paris, Harmattan, 1999.

3. The authors settled on a straightforward division of labour in Part III. The senior author was responsible for the writing of the study, while the junior author, with instruction from the senior author, collected the data, interpreted their significance and put them in 'digestible' formats.

4. The circumstances surrounding the founding of IDA have been a matter of some debate in the community of Bank students and officials. According to some, the IDA initially was not welcome by IBRD officials, who embraced it only when it became clear they could not stop the new organization. This rendering of history is disputed (see last citation below). Criticisms of IBRD in those days centred on its propensity to lend money for capital-intensive projects, especially electric power plants, and its 'high' rates of interests, which put the world's poorest countries at a disadvantage. Some thought that the IBRD practice of raising money on capital markets compelled it to pay too much attention to projects with promising rates of return, to maintain its credit rating. This meant that social development projects, such as those connected to public health, nutrition and education, might be neglected. An organization like IDA, which received money directly from the governments of member states, might be better able to deal with projects with low rates of return on investment but whose contribution to development was inestimable. The reader can see from this brief exposé that concerns about the World Bank are long-running, and have not only come from rabble rousers; there are probably few charges levelled at the Bank now (2005) that have not been levelled in the past, even the distant past, by people sympathetic to the institution. For a history of the World Bank, see Robert W. Oliver, Early Plans for a World Bank, *Studies in International Finance*, no. 29, Princeton University, September 1971. See also Alec Cairncross, The

International Bank for Reconstruction and Development, *Essays in International Finance*, no. 33, Princeton University, March 1959. For an analysis disputing the forced imposition of IDA on IBRD, see Michael Hoffman, 'The Challenges of the 1970s and the Present Institutional Structure', in John Lewis and Ishan Kapur (eds.), *The World Bank, Multilateral Aid, and the 1970s,* Princeton: Princeton University Press, 1971.

5. 'What is the World Bank?' http:/web.worldbank.org.

6. *World Bank, Lending Instruments*, Washington, D.C., The World Bank, 2000, 24.

7. If the US, UK, France, Germany and Japan do not borrow from the World Bank, it is not hard surmise what their representatives do on the board of executive directors: they influence decisions regarding the countries that do borrow from the Bank. For the Big Five representation on the board is a matter of prestige, and a way of making and maintaining friends, as well as punishing enemies, in borrowing countries.

8. Christian Aid, *Struggling to be Heard: Democratizing the World Bank and IMF*, p. 10, www.christianaid.org.uk

9. Ibid. p. 8, Clarification added in brackets by author.

10. Joseph Stiglitz reports that at the World Bank's creation, development was added to the Bank's official name—the International Bank for Reconstruction and Development—'almost as an afterthought'. Joseph Stiglitz, *Globalization and Its Discontents*, New York, W.W. Norton & Company, 2002, p. 11.

11. Robert Asher, 'Comment: The Leopard's Spots', in *The World Bank, Multilateral Aid, and the 1970s*, Princeton: Princeton University Press, 1971.

12. W.W. Rostow, *The Stages of Economic Growth: A Non-Communist Manifesto,* Cambridge, UK, Cambridge University Press, 1960. Although this book was published in 1960, it could not but be about events in the 1950s.

13. Alexander Gerschenkron, *Economic Backwardness in Historical Perspective*, Cambridge, MA, Harvard University Press, 1962.

14. One of the most influential works expounding this view was by the sociologist Daniel Lerner. See Daniel Lerner, *The Passing of Traditional Society: Modernizing the Middle East*, New York, The Free Press, 1958.

15. This view has since been challenged, if not discredited. See Samuel Popkin, *The Rational Peasant,* Berkeley, CA, University of California Press, 1979.

16. Rita Abrahamsen, *Disciplining Democracy: Development Discourse and Good Governance in Africa*, London, New York, Zed Books, 2000.

17. This is the meaning I ascribe to the following statement by Michel Foucault: 'there is no power relations without the correlative constitution of a field of knowledge, nor any knowledge that does not presuppose and constitute at the same time power relations.' Quoted in Abrahamsen, ibid. 14.

18. For an excellent critique of modernization theory, see Gilbert Rist, *The History of Development,* London and New York, Z Books, 1997, chapter 6.

19. Peter Schraeder, *African Politics and Society,* New York, St. Martin's Press, 2000.

20. Rober Ayres, 'Breaking the Bank', *Foreign Policy* 43 (Summer, 1981), p. 11.

21. Robert McNamara, *The McNamara Years at the World Bank: Major Policy Addresses of Robert S. McNamara 1968-1981,* Baltimore, MD, Johns Hopkins University Press, 1981.

22. Bank presidents enjoy enormous power. McNamara used his to steer the organization in the direction he preferred by filling key positions with like-minded people. Stiglitz, *op. cit.* p. 13.

23. Robert Ayres, *Banking on the Poor,* Cambridge, MA: MIT Press, 1983, p. 103.

24. Quoted in Peter J. Henriot, 'Development Alternatives: Problems, Strategies, Values', in Charles Wilber (ed.), *The Political Economy of Development and Underdevelopment,* New York: Random House, 1979, p. 9.

25. I came of age at the very end of this period but debates then were no less heated, certainly not at the Fernand Braudel Center at SUNY-Binghamton under the leadership of Immanuel Wallerstein.

26. David Leonard, *Reaching the Peasant Farmer,* Chicago, University of Chicago Press, 1978.

27. Samir Amin, *Unequal Development: An Essay on the Social Formation of Peripheral Capitalism,* Hassocks, Harvester Press, 1976.

28. Thandika Mkandawire, 'The Political Economy of Development with a Democratic Face', in Giovanni Cornia, Rolph van der Hoeven and Thandika Mkandawire, *Africa's Economic Recovery in the 1990s,* New York: St. Martin's Press, 1992.

29. Ibid. p. 297.

30. Hollis B. Chenery et al., *Redistribution with Growth,* Oxford, UK: Oxford University Press, 1974.

31. This is still the position of the Bank on poverty. According to What is Poverty?: 'Poverty is hunger. Poverty is lack of shelter. Poverty is being sick and not being able to see a doctor. Poverty is not being able to go to school and not

knowing how to read... Poverty is losing a child to illness brought about by unclean water...' http://www.worldbank.org/poverty/mission/up1.htm, extracted July 5, 2003.

32. John Mihevc, *The Market Tells them So*, London, UK, ZED Books, 1995, chapter 3.

33. Adebayo Olukoshi, 'The Origins, Nature and Dimensions of the African Debt Crisis', in Adebayo Olukoshi and G.O. Olusanya (eds), *The African Debt Crisis*, Lagos, Nigerian Institute of International Affairs, monograph series no. 14, 1989.

34. Akpan Ekpo, ibid.

35. Peter Gibbon, 'The World Bank and African Poverty, 1973-91', The *Journal of Modern African Studies*, Vol. 30, No. 2, 1992, pp 193-200.

36. An influential voice within the bank has been that of Ann Krueger. Her work on rent-seeking provided the justification for reforming African, and other Third World, economies, at the same time that it has been used to explain the failure of reform. For the original exposé of her thesis, see Ann Krueger, 'The Political Economy of the Rent Society', *American Economic Review*, Vol. 64, No. 3, 1974. For an excellent critique of rent-seeking and other theories on the politics of economic policy in Africa, see Thandika Mkandawire, 'The Political Economy of Development with a Human Face', op. cit.

37. Robert McNamara, *In Retrospect: The Tragedy and the Lessons of Vietnam*, New York Times, Books of Random House, 1995.

38. Adebayo Olukoshi and Liisa Laako, *Challenges to the Nation-State in Africa*, Helsinki: Institute of Development Studies, 1996.

39. Adebayo Olukoshi, 'Impact of IMF-World Bank Programmes on Nigeria', in Bade Onimode, (ed.) *The IMF, the World Bank and the African Debt,* Vol. 1, London and New Jersey: Zed Books Ltd, 1989, p. 220.

40. Cuba, in fact, almost did, but the United States greatly miscalculated the resiliency of Fidel Castro. Even more amazing, Cuba was able to survive the demise of its former patron with only minor adjustments in its ideological orientation and virtually none in its social policy. Cuba in the post-Cold War has been understudied, in part, I suspect, because it defies (for the time being) convention.

41. Edward Said, *Orientalism*, New York, Vintage Books, 1979, p. 21.

42. Peter Nicholas, 'The World Bank's Lending for Adjustment', *World Bank Discussion Papers*, Washington, D.C., The World Bank, 1988, p. 1.

43. For an excellent psycho-political analysis of the Reagan era, see Michael Rogin, *'Ronald Reagan', the Movie: and Other Episodes in Political Demonology*, Berkeley: University of California Press, 1987.

44. Peter Nicholas, op. cit. p. vii.

45. Susan George, 'Uses and Abuses of African Debt', in Adebayo Adedeji (ed.), *Africa within the World,* London and New Jersey: Zed Books, 1993.

46. Moeen Ahmed Qureshi, 'Policy-Based Lending by the World Bank', *Journal of International Development,* Vol. 3, No. 2, 1991, 101–113.

47. Peter Nicholas, op. cit. p. vii.

48. Ibid. p. viii.

49. Richard Jolly, 'Poverty and Adjustment in the 1990s', in John Lewis (ed.), *Strengthening the Poor: What Have We Learned?* New Brunswick, NJ: Transaction Books, 1988. See also Sayre Schatz, 'Structural Adjustment: A Failing Grade So Far', *Journal of Modern African Studies*, 1995, pp. 679-692. The World Bank, not surprisingly, disputes the accuracy of findings of this sort, but it is testimony to their partial veracity that the Bank has found it necessary to publish such works as Adjustment with a Human Face and Protecting the Vulnerable and Promoting Growth. See Giovanni Andrea Cornia, Richard Jolly and Frances Stewart (eds.), *Adjustment with a Human Face*, Vol. 1, Protecting the Vulnerable and Promoting Growth, Vol. 2, Oxford, UK, Oxford University Press, 1987 and 1988.

50. For a description and defence of 'Reaganomics', which has also been called supply-side economics, see Jude Wanniski, *The Way the World Works*, New York, Simon and Schuster, 1983. For a partial repudiation, see Michael Evans, The Truth About Supply-Side Economics, New York: Basic Books, 1983.

51. Milton Friedman and Anna Schwartz, *A Monetary History of the United States 1867- 1960*, Princeton: Princeton University Press, 1963.

52. On the other hand, the banking industry, whence sprang Clausen, was known to be a major contributor to the Republican Party in the United States.

53. It is one of the ironies of the World Bank and the IMF that they do business in places with which their leaders are unfamiliar — at least at the beginning of their tenure.

54. A.W. Clausen, 'Major Policy Addresses 1981-1986', in *World Bank, The Development Challenge of the Eighties,* Washington, D.C., The World Bank, 1987.

55. Readers may point to the Berg Report as the academic inspiration to SAPs. I do not share this view; the Berg Report was more of a policy report by a group of experts appointed by the World Bank than an academic exercise, which typically

involves a free flow of ideas among scholars. The Berg Report certainly cannot be put in the same mold as the debates that animated modernization theory and dependency theory in the 1960s and 1970s.

56. Robert Bates, *Markets and States in Tropical Africa: The Political Bias of Agricultural Policies*, Berkeley, University of California Press, 1981. Michael Lipton, *Why Poor People Stay Poor: Urban Bias in World Development,* Cambridge, MA.: Harvard University Press, 1977.

57. Philip Ndegwa, *Africa's Development Crisis,* Nairobi, Kenya: Heinemann Educational Books Inc., 1985, p. 54.

58. World Bank, *Accelerated Development in Sub-Saharan Africa: An Agenda for Action,* Washington, D.C., The World Bank, 1981, p. 6.

59. Jean-Germain Gros, *The Privatization of Livestock Services in Cameroun,* PhD Dissertation, Berkeley, CA, University of California at Berkeley, 1993.

60. Deji Popoola, 'Nigeria—Consequences for Health', in Aderante Adepoju (ed.), *The Impact of Structural Adjustment on the Population of Africa,* London, UK, James Currey Ltd., 1993.

61. T.O. Fadayomi, ibid. p. 99.

62. Adebayo Olukoshi, 'Impact of IMF-World Bank Programmes on Nigeria', op. cit., p. 228.

63. Ibid. p. 93.

64. I was in Cameroon in February of 1994, one month after the devaluation of the CFA Franc. I returned again in 2000. The impoverishment among some of my friends at Yaoundé University and some of the ministries had by then become very visible, but not to the World Bank, which was singling out Cameroon as a 'success', because of the ostensible return of economic growth. In Cameroon, as in many other African countries, it is not hard to know how locals are doing: the frequency with which visitors are invited for dinner, or simply a beer, either in the home or at a restaurant, is directly proportional to the well-being of the hosts. The departure of professionals and academics from Cameroon is also a very good indicator of deteriorating life conditions there.

65. Bright Okogu, 'Structural Adjustment Policies in African Countries: A Theoretical Assessment', in Bade Onimode (ed.), op. cit. 1989.

66. Akpan Ekpo, op. cit. p. 42.

67. *Africa Research Bulletin*, February 1989, pp. 9441-9442.

68. Adebayo Adedeji, Owodunni Teriba and Patrick Bugembe (eds.), *The Challenge of African Economic Recovery and Development*, London, UK, Frank Cass & Co. Ltd, 1991, p. 7.

69. United Nations Economic Commission for Africa, *African Alternative Framework to Structural Adjustment Programmes for Socio-Economic Recovery and Transformation*, Addis Ababa, UNECA, 1989, p. i.

70. Mary Turok (ed.), *The African Response: Adjustment or Transformation*, London, UK, Institute for African Alternatives, 1992.

71. World Bank, *From Crisis to Sustainable Growth*, Washington, D.C., World Bank, 1990, p. xii

72. Oladeji Ojo, 'Beyond Structural Adjustment: Policies for Sustainable Growth and Development in Africa', in Giovanni Andrea and Cornia and Gerald Helleiner (eds.), *From Adjustment to Development in Africa: Conflict, Convergence, Consensus*, London, UK, The Macmillan Press Ltd, 1994.

73. United Nations Development Program, *2004 Human Development Report*, www.undp.org.

74. Larry Elliot, 'The Lost Decade', *The Guardian*, Wednesday, July 9, 2003.

75. United Nations, *Human Development Index Annual Report 2003*, www.un.org.

76. Celia Dugger, 'Devastated by AIDS, Africa Sees Life Expectancy Plunge', *New York Times*, July 16, 2004.

77. See Jean-Germain Gros, 'Crime and Collapsed States in the Age of Globalization', *British Journal of Criminology*, Vol. 43, No. 1, 2003, pp. 63-80.

78. World Bank Development Report 1997, *The State in a Changing World*, 'Foreword', New York, Oxford University Press, 1997.

79. International Monetary Fund, Factsheet — Poverty Reduction Strategy Papers (PRSPs), http://www.imf.org/external/np/exr/facts/prsp.htm

80. Ibid.

81. Christian Aid, *op. cit.* p. 6.

82. Célestin Monga, *The Anthropology of Anger*, Boulder, CO, Lynne Rienner Publishers, 1996.

83. Victor Le Vine, *Politics in Francophone Africa*, Boulder, CO, Lynne Rienner Publishers, 2004.

84. Samuel Huntington, *Political Order in Changing Societies*, New Haven, CT, Yale University Press, 1968.

85. The late Claude Ake was, as always, very perceptive on this point. Just because African leaders said they wanted development and justified the depoliticization of political life on this ground did not mean that they really wanted development. But in the period between the end of World War II and the fall of the Berlin Wall, authoritarianism, especially the right-wing variety, was a blot western institutions, like the World Bank, and governments, not to mention certain public intellectuals, were willing to live with. Of course, the results of authoritarianism were devastating for Africa and the Third World as whole. See Claude Ake, *How Politics Underdevelops Africa*, in Adebayo Adedeji et al, *op. cit.* 1991.

86. One may ask: If SAPs were unpopular throughout Africa, which they were, why would Africans elect leaders and parties in favour of SAPs? The answer lies in the fact that few politicians in Africa were openly in favour of SAPs, and fewer still ran their campaign on faithful execution of SAPs. They could run without taking a position on SAPs, unless compelled to do so. Furthermore, politicians are not above reversing themselves, especially in a context of extreme dependency. Such is the preponderance of the World Bank (and the IMF) in many African countries that no matter who gets elected, there is unlikely to be a reversal in economic policy. Thus the National Patriotic Party (currently in power in Ghana) and the National Democratic Council (formerly in power) have pursued roughly similar Bank and IMF-sponsored economic policies. Democratization in post-Cold War Africa has had the paradoxical effect of opening the political space to opposition parties but sealing the ideological space around markets. The winners in all of this have been those (e.g., the World Bank) who prefer to limit democracy to its liberal, or non-redistributive, form.

87. Here I part company with those on the Left, who seem to think that democracy is not worth pursuing unless it leads to economic redistribution. There is some inherent value to being able to choose one's leaders, to having free speech and to worship (the latter, not a minor event for African peoples all over the world). In politics one must never make perfection the enemy of the good: liberal democracy is preferable to authoritarianism, although not as preferable as social democracy. Nor must one lose sight of the nature of social change, which is often reformist in character in the short term, but revolutionary, at least sometimes, in the longer term.

88. James March and Herbert Simon, *Organizations*, New York, John Wiley, 1958, p. 4.

89. W. Richard Scott, *Organizations – Rational, Natural, and Open Systems*, Englewood Cliffs, NJ, Prentice-Hall, 1981, p. 58.

90. Gareth Morgan, *Images of Organization*, Beverly Hills, CA, Sage, 1986.

91. Kenneth Boulding, 'General Systems Theory', *Management Science*, 2, 1956, pp. 197-208.

92. Morgan, *op. cit.* p. 45.

93. For an excellent study of the history of development as ideology, see Gilbert Rist, *The History of Development*, op. cit.

94. Amartya Sen, *Development as Freedom*, New York, Anchor Books, 2000, c1999.

95. James Thompson and Arthur Tuden, 'Strategies, Structures and Processes of Organizational Decisions' in David A. Kolb, Irwin M. Rubin and James McIntyre (eds.) *Organizational Psychology: A Book of Readings*, Englewood Cliffs, NJ: Prentice-Hall, 1971.

96. Douglas North, *Structure and Change in Economic History*, New York, W.W. Norton & Company, 1981, p. 29. Authors' words added in brackets inside the quote.

97. Empirically, of course, the notion can be easily refuted. There have been few development 'success stories' since the Industrial Revolution, including in the pioneer country of the United Kingdom, in which the state has not played a key role, either as a direct owner of productive assets or a facilitator of their acquisition, including, nay, especially, by violent means. However, this is the subject of another study.

98. North, op. cit. p. 53.

99. I am not rejecting the notion that ideology has a material basis; however, I am suggesting that the latter is dynamic rather than static, thereby giving rise to ideological change, often at the margin and less so at the core. When an ideology changes at the core, for all intent and purposes, it no longer exists, a new one takes its place.

100. World Bank, *World Bank Development Report 1997 – The State in a Changing World*, Washington, D.C.: World Bank 1997.

101. Arthur Stinchcombe, *Constructing Social Theories*, Chicago and London, University of Chicago Press, 1968.

102. This section benefits immensely from the pioneer works of Graham T. Allison and Morton Halperin, respectively: *Essence of Decision: Explaining the Cuban Missile Crisis*, Boston: Little, Brown, 1971; Bureaucratic Politics and Foreign Policy, Washington, D.C., The Brookings Institution, 1974. I recognize that their works deal with inter-agency politics in foreign policy, but if one replaces agencies with bureaus, or specialized units within the Bank, the model probably still stands, although one would expect inter-agency politics to be

sharper, and for parochial interests to be more entrenched, than in intra-agency politics — maybe.

103. I am very much aware that the negotiations that precede Bank lending take place on a case-by-case, or country-by-country, basis and that not every one at the Bank is involved in these exercises. I am talking about the major philosophical principles (e.g., SAPs) that underpin Bank lending policies every decade or so. These are not made by a lower level officials; they are often the object of internal debates among top officials, over which some people, rather than succumb to convention, have from time to time resigned.

104. Graham T. Allison and Morton Halperin, 'Bureaucratic Politics: A Paradigm and Some Policy Implications', *American Political Science Review*, Spring 1972, p. 43.

105. FAQs About the World Bank Group, http://web.worldbank.org

106. The case of Haiti is instructive. On January 6, 2005, the World Bank announced: 'Haiti: World Bank Approves $73 million for Economic Governance and Disaster Recovery Efforts in Haiti.' But somewhere toward the end of the announcement came the shocker: Haiti had to settle $52.6 million in overdue debt services to the Bank, essentially by emptying its treasury. Thus, the net disbursement to Haiti was actually far less ($20.4 million), which, no doubt, the country will soon start servicing. How many new police officers could have been trained and hired, kilometres of roads built or repaired, schools and hospitals erected in the Western Hemisphere's poorest republic?

107. This problem, I admit, is attenuated somewhat by the presence of IDA, which tends to lend to poor countries, while IBRD focuses on middle income ones.

108. This has implication for activists. It means that public pressure can be brought to bear on the Bank to change policy course, at least in some cases. It was probably pressure from environmentalists and others that led the Bank to insist on the creation of a fund into which oil receipts would be deposited and used to provide social services in Chad. This was a condition for Bank funding of the Chad-Cameroon pipeline, by which oil from Chad flows through Cameroon (via Kribi) en route to world markets.

109. For a study of Bank politicization by the United States, see Bartram Brown, *The United States and the Politicization of the World Bank*, London and New York, Kegan Paul International Ltd., 1992.

110. Chalmers Johnson, *The Sorrows of Empire*, New York: Metropolitan Books, 2004.

111. Gibbon, op. cit.

112. Jean-François Bayart, *The State in Africa: The Politics of the Belly,* London, New York, Longman, 1993.

113. Some may quibble with the notion that these project areas affect the poor more directly than others. Education funding, for example, may go toward tertiary, or higher, education, in which case it would tend to benefit middle class and elite members of society. By contrast, improvements in rural infrastructure, — for example, roads — may be of great benefit to poor farmers, who may find it easier to take their goods to market. In defence of the project areas listed in this study as being directly beneficial to the poor, we should note that they are the same ones that the Bank and international agencies normally use to measure human development. Nevertheless, we are cognizant of their imperfection as proxy measurements.

114. One person was responsible for data collection and processing — Ms. Prokopovych — and, as a graduate student research assistant to the senior co-author, strict limits were put on how much time she could spend on the project (at most, 20 hours per week).

115. An extensive discussion of how these variables are operationalized is not appropriate here.

116. In furtherance of its official interest in poverty reduction the World Bank Group created the Task Force on the Work of the World Bank Group in Low-Income Countries Under Stress. As stated in the task force's report:

> The Task Force on the Work of the World Bank Group in Low-Income Countries Under Stress was created to respond to concerns about how the development community...can best help chronically weak-performing countries get onto a path leading to sustainable growth, development, and poverty reduction (World Bank, 'World Bank Group Work in Low-Income Countries Under Stress: A Task Force Report', World Bank, Washington, D.C., September 2002.)

117. Poverty was the title of the 1990 World Bank Development Report, more or less the flagship of World Bank publications. In fact, it would be difficult to find any major Bank literature during the period under study that does not mention poverty almost in the absence breadth as that other buzzword in Bankspeak: adjustment.

118. In making comparisons between countries on the HDI scale, we thought it best to examine those that received both IDA and IBRD financing, in order to be able to make valid statements about Bank behaviour. In a more perfect world, it would have been preferable to compare the highest ranking country on the HDI (China) with the lowest ranking (Sierra Leone), the second highest with the second lowest, and so on, but, once again, there are only 6 countries in the study that reported receiving IDA and World Bank funding for the 10

project sectors from 1984 to 2004. As a substitute, we pair China (96) with Chad (166), Bolivia (114) with Pakistan (138), and Egypt (115) with India (124).

119. These results are close enough to .5 for us to say there is a correlation. The regression results, specifically the t-score (-2.10), further substantiate the case.

120. This is not surprising. Transparency International is (loosely) affiliated with the World Bank and the IMF. Many of its employees previously worked for the two agencies.

121. Tatah Mentan, 'Cameroon: the Political Economy of Poverty', in Jean-Germain Gros (ed.), *Cameroon – Politics and Society in Critical Perspectives,* Lanham, MD: University Press of America, 2003.

122. However, a Bank-sponsored effort to 'encourage' veterinarians to leave government and set up private practice failed. Livestock farmers were willing to buy drugs and treat their animals, rather than take them to vets. Simply put, there was not a market for private veterinarians other than as drug sellers, at least not in the Cameroon countryside. In the cities of Douala, Yaoundé, etc., such a market existed, especially for domestic pets, but Cameroon veterinarians did not need the World Bank to tell them that.

123. Joseph Stiglitz, 'Democratizing the International Monetary Fund and the World Bank, *Governance and Accountability',* *Governance: An International Journal of Policy, Administration and Institutions,* Vol. 16, No. 1, 2003, pp. 111-139.

124. Christian Aid, op. cit. p. 7

125. Ibid. p. 12.

126. Susan Holcombe, *Managing to Empower: the Grameen Bank's Experience of Poverty Alleviation,* Atlantic Highlands, NJ : Zed Books, 1995.

www.ingramcontent.com/pod-product-compliance
Lightning Source LLC
Chambersburg PA
CBHW030656270326
41929CB00007B/393